HOUSE of DREAMS

HOUSE of DREAMS
The Life of L. M. Montgomery

Liz Rosenberg

illustrated by Julie Morstad

CANDLEWICK PRESS

First edition 2018

Library of Congress Catalog Card Number pending
ISBN 978-0-7636-6057-4

18 19 20 21 22 23 LSC 10 9 8 7 6 5 4 3 2 1

Printed in Crawfordsville, IN, U.S.A.

This book was typeset in Garamond.
The illustrations were done in ink.

Candlewick Press
99 Dover Street
Somerville, Massachusetts 02144

visit us at www.candlewick.com

For Eli and Anna,
and the great love between them.
And for Lily, of course, this book's first reader.
And for Lois, kindred spirit.
L. R.

TABLE OF CONTENTS

CHAPTER ONE

A Bend in the Road

On a late June afternoon in 1905, Maud Montgomery sat in her grandmother's kitchen, writing. She sat not *at* the kitchen table, but perched on top of it, her feet set neatly on a nearby sofa, her notebook propped against her knees. From here she could jump down if someone stopped by for their mail, as was likely to happen—for the kitchen doubled as the post office of Cavendish, a tiny seaside village on Prince Edward Island.

Maud was thirty, but she looked younger, barely out of her teens. She had large, sparkling gray-blue eyes with long eyelashes, and a small mouth she sometimes covered with her hand, since she thought her teeth her worst feature. She was medium height, slight, trim, and erect. Maud believed her one beauty to be her lustrous hair, a feature she'd inherited from her late mother. When she let it down at night, her hair hung past her knees in masses of soft brown waves. But most of the time she wore it up, pinned under the most fanciful and elaborate hats she could find.

At this moment Maud was working on a new story. Though she had just begun, she felt immediately transported to another world—a Cavendish-like place she would call Avonlea. Something about this story and its eager, orphaned heroine ("please call me Anne spelled with an *e*") gripped Maud from the start. The words flowed smoothly onto her notebook. Her handwriting was never stronger or more sure. Maud began her tale not with her famous red-haired heroine but with the town of Avonlea itself and the sharp-eyed Mrs. Lynde who guards it. Maud wrote in one rushing paragraph-long opening sentence:

Mrs. Rachel Lynde lived just where the Avonlea main road dipped down into a little hollow, fringed with alders and ladies' eardrops and traversed by a brook that had its source away back in the woods of the old Cuthbert place; it was reputed to be an intricate, headlong brook in its earlier course through those woods, with dark secrets of pool and cascade; but by the time it reached

Lynde's Hollow it was a quiet, well-conducted little stream, for not even a brook could run past Mrs. Rachel Lynde's door without due regard for decency and decorum; it probably was conscious that Mrs. Rachel was sitting at her window, keeping a sharp eye on everything that passed, from brooks and children up, and that if she noticed anything odd or out of place she would never rest until she had ferreted out the whys and wherefores thereof.

The day was dazzling after rain, and Maud sat in the late sunlight flooding in. Her moods were like the weather—brilliant one minute, overcast the next. June was Maud's favorite month. You could practically count her happiness by Junes. She wrote about it more than all the other months combined, naming each of its beauties. When spring finally swept the north shore of Prince Edward Island, Maud abandoned her small, dark "winter bedroom" off the downstairs parlor and moved upstairs, where she could write and dream uninterruptedly. No one else ventured up there; hidden, Maud was queen and sole resident of her springtime domain. But now she was working out in the open, intent on her new story, her pen racing to catch up to her thoughts.

She had just reached the point where nosy Mrs. Lynde wonders at her shy neighbor, Matthew Cuthbert, heading out with the buggy and sorrel mare, wearing his best suit:

"Now, where was Matthew Cuthbert going and why was he going there?"

Just at this moment, Maud was interrupted. The new minister in town, Ewan Macdonald, stopped by for his mail. Maud set her writing aside. Ewan was a shy, gentle bachelor who had lately moved to Cavendish, taking a room within walking distance of the Presbyterian Church, next door to the Macneill homestead, her grandparents' house. He was a frequent visitor to the post office. To Maud, the young minister seemed a bit lonely. He was well educated, with hopeful prospects. Ewan Macdonald attracted local attention with his dark wavy hair, dimples, and lilting Gaelic accent. The accent was especially appealing to Maud, since she'd grown up hearing romantic tales of Scotland, the Old Country.

A handsome unmarried minister was a natural target for local gossip. The Cavendish girls were rumored to be "crazy about him," and more than a few threw themselves in Ewan's path. Maud was not one of them. She liked the shy Scotsman and enjoyed his company, but she was not looking for a suitor. She'd already had a few too many ardent proposals, but she was always hungry for a new friend. Maud welcomed the new minister's company, and kept the conversation light. If she felt flattered—or interested—she didn't let on, and that was a relief for Ewan Macdonald, who had just escaped a near marriage to an overeager woman in another town.

The Macneills had been staunch Presbyterians as far back as anyone could remember. Maud was the church organist; she was merry, she was bright, and she and Ewan had plenty to talk about. Ewan lingered as long as daylight held out; only when the kitchen grew dappled with shadows did he reluctantly leave with his letters. Maud picked up her notebook and carried it upstairs.

She had come to a bend in the road—though at that moment she could not see around it. It seemed merely the end of a vibrant June day. She had a new friend in town, and she had begun a new story. Maud had no way of knowing that absolutely everything in her life was about to change.

CHAPTER TWO

An Early Sorrow

Lucy Maud Montgomery—"call me Maud without an *e*," she would insist, discarding the use of Lucy altogether—grew up proud of her long, deep roots in the history of Prince Edward Island.

On cold Canadian nights, the Macneill family gathered around the kitchen stove and talked. And talked. Little Maud sat at the knee of her great-aunt Mary Lawson, wide-eyed. Aunt Mary Lawson was a wonderful storyteller. Tales of ancient grudges, courtships, and adventures were discussed as eagerly as that morning's gossip. Those old stories provided the first clues to Maud about who she came from, and who she might become. She never forgot them. Maud came to know her Prince Edward Island ancestors as well as she knew her own neighbors.

In the 1700s Maud's seasick great-great-grandmother Mary Montgomery came aground at Prince Edward Island for a few minutes' relief, and then, to her husband's horror, refused to board ship again. He could beg and plead and fume, but she would not budge. Right there on Prince Edward Island they would and did stay. Maud's family history began on the heels of one stubborn, seasick, strong-willed woman.

The Montgomerys traced their lineage back to the Scottish Earl of Eglinton—a dubious connection, but one Maud's father clung to. (He would one day name his own house Eglintoun Villa.) Maud's paternal grandfather, Donald Montgomery, was a staunch Conservative. Among his friends he counted the first prime minister of Canada and leading members of the Conservative Party. Donald Montgomery served in the Prince Edward Island legislature for more than forty years and then in the Senate another twenty till his death at age eighty-six. He was known simply as "the Senator."

The Senator kept on his mantel two large china dogs with green spots. According to Maud's father, each midnight they would leap down from the shelf to the hearthrug. The story—and the spotted china dogs—enchanted little Maud. As patiently as she watched, she never caught them coming alive. But she never forgot them, either. Years later, on her honeymoon, when she spied two large spotted china dogs for sale, she snapped them up and shipped them home to guard her bookcase. They were vivid, proud reminders of her father's side of the family.

On Maud's maternal side, the Macneills were equally well-known and respected—all of them dedicated Liberals, or Grits. This put them directly in political opposition to the Montgomerys. In this and in much else, Maud would find herself torn between two powerful and contradictory forces.

Maud's maternal great-great-grandmother Elizabeth was as stubborn as the seasick one—but less successful at swaying her husband. She hated Prince Edward Island. "Bitterly homesick she was—rebelliously so. For weeks after her arrival she would not take off her bonnet, but walked the floor in it, imperiously demanding to be taken home. We children who heard the tale never wearied of speculating as to whether she took off her bonnet at night and put it on again in the morning, or whether she slept in it."

Maud's home village of Cavendish, on the central north coast of Prince Edward Island, was founded in the late 1700s by three Scottish families: the Macneills, the Simpsons, and the Clarks. By Maud's day, she noted, these three important families "had intermarried to such an extent that it was necessary to be born or bred in

Cavendish in order to know whom it was safe to criticize." There was a tart local saying about these families: "From the conceit of the Simpsons, the pride of the Macneills, and the vain-glory of the Clarks good Lord deliver us."

Maud came from the "proud" Macneills. She claimed that her "knack of writing . . . and literary tastes" sprang from this maternal side of the family. Her maternal great-grandfather, William Simpson Macneill, was a powerful Speaker of the House—it was said that he knew by name every man, woman, and child on Prince Edward Island. Even his portrait looked so formidable that one of his successors, still intimidated by it one hundred years later, finally had it taken down and hidden away.

One of the Speaker's eleven children became a noted politician, another a well-known lawyer, but Alexander Macneill, Maud's grandfather, was simply a farmer and the local postmaster. It was said he had possessed many of the Speaker's best qualities—eloquence, dignity, intelligence—but also his weaknesses to a serious degree. Grandfather Macneill was proud, sharp-tongued, tyranni-cal, and hypersensitive. He picked fights with family and neighbors that turned into long-term feuds.

Undoubtedly Grandfather Macneill was proud of his clever granddaughter Maud, but his method was to praise in private and bully or ridicule in public. Maud had to learn from her cousins that her fierce grandfather whispered complimentary things behind her back.

She shrank from Grandfather Macneill's razor wit. Maud hated the way he mocked and belittled her—and he couldn't help doing it. Her most famous literary creation, Anne Shirley, shares her aversion: "sarcasm, in man or woman, was the one weapon Anne dreaded. It always hurt her . . . raised blisters on her soul that smarted for months." Likewise, Maud's fictional Story Girl vows never to make fun of a child: ". . . it IS hateful to be laughed at—and grown-ups always do it. I never will when I'm grown up. I'll remember better."

Maud was proud of her family, but her legacy was far from easy. Both sides were fully convinced of the rightness of their ways. Maud knew that she had inherited qualities from the Montgomerys and the Macneills destined to be forever at odds: "the passionate Montgomery blood and the Puritan Macneill conscience." She also understood that neither side was "strong enough wholly to control the other." The two sides battled it out endlessly in Maud's double nature.

Maud put a brave face to the world, protecting and hiding the inner Maud. "I lived my double life, as it seems to me I have always done—as many people do, no doubt—the outward life of study and work . . . and the inner one of dreams and aspirations."

Maud's life began in joy but turned to early sorrow. Both the joy and the sorrow left their mark. Lucy Maud

Montgomery was born November 30, 1874, in the Prince Edward Island town of Clifton—later renamed New London—in a tiny two-floor cottage, eight and a half months after her parents' wedding.

Her father, Hugh John Montgomery, was thirty-three years old, the handsome, merry, likable but unlucky son of Senator Donald Montgomery. When Hugh John first met Maud's mother, Clara Woolner Macneill, he cut a dashing figure as a young sea captain. Ever the optimist, he swept all opposition aside to claim his young bride.

Clara Woolner Macneill was a young woman of twenty-one, the fourth of her parents' six well-protected children. In the little village of Cavendish, Clara stood out. She turned heads with her beauty, and won more than one suitor's heart. In later years, a gray-haired man approached Maud and shyly bragged that he had once had the honor of walking her mother home.

Clara and Hugh John were married in her parents' parlor, but the elder Macneills never really approved the match. Hugh John seemed unlikely to become a good provider. Hugh John's father, Senator Donald Montgomery, bought the young couple a small cottage on Prince Edward Island, halfway between the two sets of parents.

The young couple struggled to make a living by running a country store attached to their living quarters. Neither husband nor wife was good at business. The store floundered. And all too soon, Clara fell ill with tuberculosis — or consumption, as it was then called — a slow, dreadful, and often fatal lung illness.

Hugh John moved to Cavendish, where the Macneills could help care for their daughter and infant granddaughter, Maud. Despite all their vigilance and attention, Clara Macneill Montgomery died on September 14, 1876, leaving behind one baby daughter and a grieving husband and family. She was twenty-three years old. Maud was not yet two. Her first memory was of her young mother lying in a coffin, her golden-brown hair spilling around her shoulders.

Hugh John stood by the casket, cradling Maud in his arms and crying. The tiny girl was bewildered: a crowd had gathered, she was the center of attention, yet something was wrong. Neighbors whispered to one another and looked at them pityingly.

Women in Maud's day owned only one silk dress in their lifetime, usually in some sensible, muted color; Clara's silk was a vivid green. Maud's mother looked glamorous even in death. With her mass of wavy golden-brown hair, she seemed as lovely and familiar as ever. But when Maud reached out to touch her mother's face, she was shocked by her ice-cold skin, a sensation so strong that years later Maud could feel it searing her fingertips.

After the funeral, a veil of silence fell over Clara Macneill Montgomery's brief life. Maud had to cobble together an image of her mother through snatches of overheard conversation and dropped hints. It was as if her mother had been erased.

From the few accounts Maud could glean, Clara had been a sensitive, poetical, high-minded, and dreamy young woman. It took courage for her to defy her parents and marry against their wishes. Maud and Clara stood out from their little clan. Both loved beauty to a degree that was considered almost madness. Maud forever mourned the loss of her mother. Though Clara died young and unknown, she left behind a few items that Maud treasured all her life—a few volumes of poetry, a daybook that Maud carefully preserved.

Clara's grave lay just across the road from Maud's house and the Presbyterian Church, beside the schoolhouse. Her mother's absence was always in sight: aching, mysterious, and unforgettable. Maud crossed through her mother's graveyard on her way to and from school each day.

Clara's early death left Maud with unanswered questions. Though the Macneill family was famous for storytelling, no stories about her mother came Maud's way. Nor did anyone sit down with Maud to discuss a possible afterlife. She was left to draw her own conclusions.

At age four, Maud was in church when the minister said something that made her sit up and take notice. One was never supposed to speak in church, of course, but this was urgent. Maud turned to her aunt Emily and piped, "Where is Heaven?"

Young Aunt Emily was too proper to answer aloud. Instead she pointed her finger up toward the ceiling. From this gesture, Maud concluded that her mother was somehow stuck in the attic of the Clifton church. Heaven was only a few miles from home! Maud could not understand why someone didn't get a ladder and fetch her mother down.

Meanwhile, Maud's home life with her father grew more insecure. Hugh John grieved for his young wife, and as he struggled to make a living, he left the care of his active young daughter to the Macneills, who were in their fifties, well past their years of child rearing. Only their teenage daughter, Maud's prim aunt Emily, still lived at home. Maud thought of her young aunt as ancient. "Either you were a grown-up or you were not, that was all there was about it." Aunt Emily was no sort of playmate, so Maud invented her own playfellows, even in the glass doors of a cupboard in her grandparents' parlor.

In the left-hand door dwelled Maud's imaginary friend, Katie Maurice. Katie was a little girl Maud's own age, to whom she would chatter "for hours, giving and receiving confidences." Maud could never poke her head into the parlor without at least waving her hand at Katie Maurice.

On the right side of the cupboard door lived the

imaginary Lucy Gray, an elderly widow who always told "dismal stories of her troubles." Maud much preferred the imaginary company of Katie Maurice, but in order to spare the feelings of the sad old widow, she was careful to spend equal time chatting to both.

Much later, Maud would bring just the favorite of her two invented friends to *Anne of Green Gables,* where Katie Maurice became Anne's imaginary first best friend and comforter.

The real-life companion of Maud's earliest childhood was her father, Hugh John. Maud worshipped him. He was gentle and merry, and he told delightful stories — like the one about his father's spotted china dogs coming to life at midnight. Maud's father praised and petted her and, unlike the Macneills, expressed himself in ways that were openly affectionate. Hugh John called her his "little Maudie," and in return she loved him unconditionally.

Years later she wrote, "I loved my father very very deeply. He was the most lovable man I ever knew." Hugh John Montgomery was childlike in his aversion to unpleasantness. Father and daughter clung to each other in a bewildering world. In her journal entry of May 3, 1908, she wrote,

> *I think now that grandfather and grandmother resented this very love of mine for him. They saw that I did not turn to them with the outgush of affection I gave him.*

And it was true—I did not. But it was their own fault.
I know now that they loved me after a fashion. But they
never expressed or showed that love in word or action. I
never thought they loved me. I felt that the only person
in the world who loved me was father. Nobody else ever
kissed and caressed me and called me pet names. So I
gave all my love to him in those years. And my grand-
parents did not like it. They thought that, as they were
giving me a home and food and clothes and care that I
ought to have loved them best.

Little Maud was a moody, active, clever, and excitable child. None of these qualities were valued by the stern Macneills. Maud yearned for open expressions of tenderness—as when a family friend, looking in on her one night, murmured, "dear little child," a phrase Maud remembered and cherished all her life. Displays of overt affection like these were rare. "And I loved such expression. I craved it. I have never forgotten it."

There is no doubt that Maud's grandmother loved her. Lucy Macneill was the central figure in Maud's life. Grandmother Macneill stood up to her husband on Maud's behalf, defied convention for her granddaughter's sake, spent her own pocket money for Maud's benefit, and fought to make sure the girl got a good education. She did all these things at a time when such behavior was the exception, not the rule. Lucy Macneill took excellent care of Maud materially—she was a famed housekeeper with skills at cooking, cleaning, and handicrafts—but emotionally and intellectually they remained miles apart.

It was as difficult for Grandmother Macneill as it was natural for Hugh John to openly express affection. But while Maud easily forgave her father many failings, she judged her grandmother harshly. Only in fiction, in the much-altered character of Marilla Cuthbert, did Maud ever celebrate her grandmother's good qualities: her reliability, self-sacrifice, her steadfast attention.

There is a little-known episode in Maud's early childhood, touched on in her Autobiographical Sketches, that suggests that once upon a time, Grandmother Macneill did hold a treasured place in her heart. At age five Maud burned herself with a poker, and the next day fell ill with typhoid fever. The doctor declared she would not survive the week. Grandmother Macneill was summoned at once.

The high-strung little girl threw herself at her grandmother. In fact, Maud was "so delighted to see her that the excitement increased my fever to an alarming pitch." In an effort to calm his daughter, Hugh John fibbed that her grandmother had gone home, and over the next feverish days Maud believed that the elderly woman hovering anxiously was not her grandmother at all, but one of the housekeepers. Only when she was well enough to sit up by herself did she see that Grandmother Lucy Macneill remained at her side. Maud wrote, "I . . . could not bear to be out of her arms. I kept stroking her face constantly and saying in amazement and delight, 'Why you're *not* Mrs. Murphy, after all; you *are* Grandma.'"

Not long after Maud's bout with typhoid fever, Grandmother Lucy Macneill became the little girl's chief caretaker. Grandmother was stern and rule-bound. Her child-rearing techniques seemed to Maud hopelessly old-fashioned. Over the next few years all the burden of parenting fell upon Grandmother Macneill. Hugh John ventured farther and farther afield into Western Canada in search of business. The once-adoring relationship vanished without a trace.

At first Hugh John made visits home to see his little daughter. But by the time Maud turned seven, her father had moved to far-off Saskatchewan, and the elderly Macneills had taken on the full care of their granddaughter.

Maud hid the shock and disappointment of her father's abandonment and redirected her rage where it could safely rest, with her ever-vigilant, elderly grandparents. Not then or later did Maud utter a word against her "darling" father, Hugh John. Quite the opposite—she created a loving portrait of the absent father that has bewildered every biographer.

It didn't help that prickly Grandfather Macneill openly opposed the new childcare arrangement, or that he was so often at odds with his talkative, temperamental grand-daughter. Alexander Macneill shrank from the world; Maud craved sociability. He scorned her flights of imagination, scoffed at her ambitions, and insisted a woman's place was in the home.

Grandmother Lucy Macneill, caught between these two strong personalities, had to play the peacemaker — she worked hard to restore order and balance to her grand-daughter's life. Trying to play fair, she pleased neither.

Maud knew that her grandmother meant well, "but her love never had the slightest saving grace of under-standing," and so, she once wrote, "had no power to draw us together." Maud had been orphaned by one parent and abandoned by the other. Another child might have been farmed out to foster care, shuttled from house to house, or sent to an orphanage, but Maud had a secure roof over her head, plenty of good food, all the material advantages at her grandparents' disposal.

The Macneills' house was one of the nicest old homes in Cavendish. Cherry and apple orchards bloomed each June, and the fruit ripened each fall. The other children brought their simple lunches to school in tin pails; Maud came home at noon and dined with her grandparents. Many children could not afford shoes even in the harsh Canadian winter; Maud wore sturdy leather boots that were the envy of all the other girls. Maud admitted,

"Materially, I was well cared for . . . It was emotionally and socially that my nature was starved and restricted."

Maud's relatives constantly reminded her that she should be grateful for her good fortune. She was a charity case. She should act thankful for the roof over her head. Nothing Maud did escaped public notice, and more would be expected of her than of any mere mortal.

CHAPTER THREE

"Very Near to a Kingdom of Ideal Beauty"

The Macneill farm sat just outside the limits of Cavendish, a seaside village of close-knit connections. The whole settlement was about three miles long and one mile wide. Cavendish lay on the rural north shore of Prince Edward Island, eleven miles from a railway station and twenty-four miles from Charlottetown. Maud considered Cavendish the most beautiful place on earth. In one rare case of understatement she called it "a good place in which to spend a childhood. I can think of none better."

In an early diary entry, Maud noted,

> *Away down beyond the brown fields lay the sea, blue and sparkling, dotted by crests of foam. The walk in*

*the fresh moist spring air was lovely and when I got down
to the shore and climbed out on a big rock I just held
my breath with delight. . . . To my left extended the
shining curve of the sand shore; and on my right were
rugged rocks with little coves, where the waves swished
on the pebbles. I could have lingered there for hours and
watched the sea with the gulls soaring over it.*

One can hear in the voice of the teenage Maud the
stirrings of the brilliant descriptive writer that she would
become.

Maud was fiercely passionate about Cavendish, her
childhood home base. However much she might privately
criticize the village, she never let an outsider say a word
against it. No place was harder to leave. None moved her
so powerfully. "It is and ever must be hallowed ground to
me," she declared. Maud knew each field and hill, the fruit
orchards, groves from which the children would gather
chews of spicy spruce gum. "I was very near to a kingdom
of ideal beauty," she claimed.

During Maud's youth, Prince Edward Island was a
tightly knit place, home to one hundred thousand people.
It was the smallest of Canada's provinces, an outly-
ing region glimmering off the eastern shore of New
Brunswick. As far as Maud was concerned, Prince Edward
Island remained "the most beautiful place in America."

Very rarely as a young child did Maud ever venture

beyond the outskirts of tiny Cavendish. Her grandparents were dedicated homebodies, and over the years they withdrew still more. A trip to Charlottetown, less than twenty-five miles away, "was a very rare treat, once in three years, and loomed up in about the same proportions of novelty, excitement, and delight as a trip to Europe would now."

It was on one such rare trip to Charlottetown that the four-year-old Maud managed to escape her grandparents for a few minutes. While Grandmother and Grandfather Macneill engaged in conversation, Maud seized her chance to explore the street alone. She was amazed to see a woman shaking out her rugs from "the top of a house." She chatted briefly with a strange girl with black eyes and black braids and felt she had had an extraordinary adventure.

Family visits to Maud's uncle John's and aunt Annie Campbell's house at nearby Park Corner happened perhaps once or twice in a year. These visits, too, Maud treasured as a welcome escape from the dour Macneill home. Maud found her first companionship at Park Corner. Here lived a "trio of merry cousins," including her younger cousin Frede Campbell, who later became Maud's closest friend, "my more than sister, the woman who was nearest and dearest to me in the world!"

There was no stiffness or formality at Park Corner, where the "heart-hungry" girl found warmth and laughter, and creature comforts — including "a famous old pantry, always stored with goodies" the cousins would raid at night, devouring "unholy snacks with sounds of riot and mirth." The big white house charmed Maud, with its nooks and cupboards and "unexpected flights of stairs." The Campbell cousins stayed awake till all hours, playing games, cracking nuts, telling jokes and stories. Uncle John and Aunt Annie joined in the merriment. Maud wrote, "I love the old spot better than any place on earth."

Maud's joy was nourished at lively Park Corner, but her soul was forged in the quiet sobriety of the Macneill homestead in Cavendish. It remained her house of dreams, her measure for all else. "Were it not for those Cavendish years . . . I do not think *Anne of Green Gables* would ever have been written," she declared. Her childhood home brought a checkered happiness, to be sure, but she clung to it passionately. "The only home my inmost soul would ever acknowledge would be that little country settlement by the gulf shore. . . ."

Maud had a fierce determination to be happy, even as a child who had tasted tragedy young. She loved to laugh and be "merry"—one of her favorite words. She had a genius for finding the fun in every situation. When there was no human company, she invented it—in the form of her imaginary friends, and in the natural beauty all around her. She was especially fond of trees, and gifted them with names and personalities. "If I believe seriously in the doctrine of transmigration," she once wrote to a friend,

"I should think I had been a tree in some previous stage of existence."

"I like things to have handles," she admitted—even something as humble as a potted geranium. Like her famous heroine Anne, Maud named every loved object from earliest childhood. She gave the trees in her grandparents' yard fanciful names: Little Syrup, the White Lady, the Monarch of the Forest. At times her vivid imagination ran away with her: a scalloped glass vase seemed to have a terrifying expression, and Maud once fancied all the chairs in her grandmother's dim parlor were dancing around the table making faces at her.

Maud had cats for company as well. All her life she owned at least one. Later, she autographed her books with a drawing of a black cat underneath her signature. "You are never poor," she declared, "as long as you've got something to love." When she wasn't busy with imaginary friends, Maud played with her kittens. Her first two cats were Pussywillow and Catkins. When Pussywillow was a kitten she ate some rat poison and died. Five-year-old Maud was heartbroken; her grandparents could not understand the little girl's wild grief. At that moment, suffering and death became real for Maud. Maud wrote that she had been "a happy, unconscious little animal. From that time I began to have a soul."

By the time Maud entered the local one-room

schoolhouse at age six, she had mastered two accomplishments. She could wiggle her ears, and she could read. There is no record of how the schoolmaster regarded the first trick, but he was clearly impressed by the second. He marched Maud to the front of the classroom and admonished the older children, "This little girl is much younger than you and already she can read better than any of you."

But her pride was quickly thrown down. On her second day of school, she arrived late and had to enter the schoolroom alone. She was keenly aware of everyone staring. "Very shyly I slipped in and sat down beside a 'big girl.' At once a wave of laughter rippled over the room. *I had come in with my hat on.*" Even writing about it forty years later, "the fearful shame and humiliation I endured at that moment rushes over me again. I felt that I was a target for the ridicule of the universe. Never, I felt certain, could I live down such a dreadful mistake. I crept out to take off my hat, a crushed morsel of humanity."

Nor was this the last time that Maud would feel publicly humiliated.

I remember one winter I was sent to school wearing a new style of apron. I think still that it was rather ugly. Then I thought it was hideous. It was a long, sack-like garment, with sleeves. Nobody in school had ever

28

worn aprons with sleeves before. . . . One of the girls sneeringly remarked that they were baby *aprons. This capped all! . . . To the end of their existence, and they* did *wear horribly well, those "baby" aprons marked for me the extreme limit of human endurance.*

Readers of *Anne of Green Gables* will remember Anne's desperate desire to look fashionable and to wear great "puffed sleeves" like the other girls. Here, as in so much of her work, Maud could draw from the details of her life, turn them upside down (from having to wear "baby sleeves" to longing for puffed sleeves), and invest them with humor and pathos. She never lost her keen sense of the pangs of childhood, later observing in *Anne of Windy Poplars,* "Isn't it queer that the things we writhe over at night are seldom wicked things? Just humiliating ones."

The one-room Cavendish school was tiny by modern standards. Even the schoolteacher stayed the same from year to year. A newcomer provided an exciting change of pace. Maud once "bought" the rights to sit beside a new girl in school. The cost for a new seatmate was four juicy apples from her grandfather's orchard. Maud considered this trade a bargain. It turned out that the new pupil was Amanda Macneill, a distant relation known as Mollie, who soon became Maud's best childhood friend.

Maud and Mollie were known as a single entity,

Mollie-and-Polly. The two little girls' personalities complemented each other. Maud was intellectual, strong-willed, and high-strung. Mollie was sweet-natured, kind, and easygoing—as gentle as Maud was fierce. Together they made mischief at school, formed clubs with other girls, shared the secrets of their first romances, and clung together through every childhood storm.

Though Maud seldom admired her Cavendish schoolmasters, she was eager to learn, and could never get enough of books. The setting of the school was a great part of its charm for the girl who spent much of her time gazing out the window. To the west and south spread an old spruce grove, where the children wandered freely at lunchtime and picked chews of gum. "I shall always be thankful that my school was near a grove—a place with winding paths and treasure-trove of ferns and mosses and wood-flowers. It was a stronger and better educative influence in my life than the lessons learned at the desk in the school-house."

Teachers, Maud found, were often strict when they should have been kind, and careless when they should have been firm. If the schoolmaster thought you knew the answer, he wouldn't call on you. If he sensed you were unprepared, he'd pounce. Maud learned to look reluctant when she really wanted to be called on and knowledgeable when lost.

* * *

Maud longed to bring a lunch pail to school and eat with her school chums, and to run barefoot with the poorer children. Maud felt like an outsider. An orphan—even a semi-orphan like Maud—was an object of general pity, scorn, and distrust. Sometimes she acted superior, but deep down Maud feared she must be unlikable. "I received an impression . . . that everybody disliked me and that I was a very hateful person." She was cleverer, better fed, and better dressed than many of her school chums—and lonelier.

Maud's desires and ambitions seemed suspect to her neighbors and relations. What did she want? What was she up to now? There was money in the Macneill household for leather boots, but little spared for the books Maud craved. Magazines came her way now and then by way of her grandparents' post office, and the beauty-hungry Maud would pore over those fashion magazines for hours.

Browsing in the sparse Macneill home library, Maud devoured the *Godey's Lady's Book* and a two-volume red-clothed *History of the World*. Hans Christian Andersen's tales provided "a perpetual joy." But fiction in general was frowned upon as reading material for children. Her grandparents owned only a handful of novels, including Dickens's *The Pickwick Papers*, Sir Walter Scott's *Rob Roy*, and Bulwer-Lytton's *Zanoni*. Little Maud read these precious, scant volumes so often that before she turned seven she claimed she had memorized entire chapters by heart.

Luckily, Maud was allowed a good deal of poetry: Shakespeare, Longfellow, Tennyson, Whittier, Scott, Milton, and Burns. But on Sundays even poetry was banned. The only permissible books, besides sermons, were religious tomes.

Maud's favorite among these was a thin, preachy volume called *A Memoir of Anzonetta R. Peters,* about a sickly girl who dies young, speaking only from scriptures and hymns. To imitate her, Maud wrote "hymn after hymn" in her diary, and patterned her own style on Anzonetta's remarks. Maud wrote that she wished she were "in Heaven now, with Mother . . . and Anzonetta R. Peters." In fact, she "didn't really wish it. I only thought I ought to." Maud tried imitating Anzonetta for a while, but soon gave it up. Anzonetta was voiceless — she spoke only through sacred texts. And Maud knew early on that she longed to express herself through writing. "I cannot remember the time when I was not writing, or when I did not mean to be an author."

Maud's artistic dreams would have been enough to brand her an oddity in Cavendish. Well-bred girls became housekeepers, not artists. They were wives and mothers, or at most they took a turn at being teachers and shopkeepers from financial necessity. They did not set their hearts on anything as frivolous as writing books.

Her relatives and neighbors might have looked more

kindly on Maud's ambitions had she set out to become a minister's wife. There, her intelligence and bookishness could have seemed an asset. But Maud decided early that she was unsuited to any formal religious life. She associated religion with grim fear and long lists of rules.

Maud was raised within the Scottish Presbyterian Church, the church of her ancestors. In the 1870s and 1880s, there were about thirty thousand Presbyterians on Prince Edward Island, and only five thousand High Church Anglicans. Any other religion was virtually unknown. Maud was subjected to terrifying fire-and-brimstone sermons, and so "suffered from spasms of fear about Hell." In the summer Maud's mind remained untroubled. But in the depths of winter, she would undergo fits of dread, and then deprive herself of even simple pleasures. She'd set the supper table giving herself a particular piece of bent silverware that she detested. To the elegance-loving Maud, this was heavy penance indeed.

A photograph of Maud taken around this time shows an otherworldly-looking girl, thin and pale, with a small mouth and enormous, sad eyes. When Maud was six, her grandmother saw in the newspaper a prediction that the world was going to end the following Sunday. Maud maintained a young child's "pathetic faith in the wisdom of grown-ups." When her grandmother read the dire prediction aloud, Maud was terror-stricken. Grown-ups never lied. The *newspaper* never lied. Try as she might, she could not stop worrying about it.

Maud held "a most absolute and piteous belief in everything that was 'printed.'" If a thing was written down and published it *must* be true. All week she badgered her aunt Emily, asking piteously if they would be going to church that Sunday. Stiffly, Aunt Emily assured Maud that they would. That "was a considerable comfort. . . . If she really expected that there would be Sunday-school she could not believe that the next day would see the end of the world."

When Maud turned seven, her grandparents threw one final public celebration at home, their last hurrah before withdrawing from Cavendish society. It was the wedding of Aunt Emily, their youngest daughter. Maud remembered the event vividly, with everyone present from both sides of her family. She memorized every detail, as if knowing it was the last glimpse of something precious.

Aunt Emily's brown silk wedding dress featured pleats and flounces and ruches and an overskirt. The bride wore a bonnet, too—jet-black with a white feather. There was dancing and feasting. Maud remembered her uncle John Montgomery keeping things lively, and it all stayed clear in her mind, because it was the last time happy crowds gathered in the old homestead. Once Aunt Emily left as a bride, the Macneills retired from society—and seven-year-old Maud was forced to retire along with them.

CHAPTER FOUR

The Jolly Years

After Aunt Emily's wedding followed a few dull months, when it seemed to Maud that nothing exciting would ever happen again. And then, suddenly, the near-miraculous occurred. Did Grandmother Lucy sense her loneliness? We'll never know for sure.

Maud's grandparents agreed to board two orphan boys of six and seven. Their names were Wellington and David Nelson, nicknamed Well and Dave. Well was just one week younger than Maud; his brother, Dave, a year younger. Maud had always longed for a sibling, and now, out of the blue, she had not one but two companions. For four glorious years Well and Dave lived with Maud's grandparents. Maud called these "the brightest and happiest memories of my childhood." She might still get into scrapes—indeed she often would—but Maud no longer got into them alone.

Dave, the younger, was fair-haired with deceptively mild, round blue eyes. Well was dark and handsome, "with laughing eyes and a merry face." Dave was never happier than when tinkering with tools and scraps of metal or wood. He was a natural engineer who loved putting things together and taking them apart. Well was bright and academic-minded, a reader almost as avid as Maud herself. Together they pored over fairy tales, ghost stories, and classics.

Neither boy ever quarreled with Maud, but both were hotheaded and fell into frequent tussles with each other. Dave always got the worst of these battles. He'd lose his temper so he could barely see straight. His fair skin would glow bright red, earning him the nickname Rooster. As quickly as the brothers came to blows, they'd make up again, and ten minutes after a battle they'd be hugging each other and rolling around like puppies. Fighting was a form of play to them—"a positive enjoyment," Maud declared.

Grandfather Macneill usually put a quick stop to this kind of pleasure. But one winter evening Grandmother Lucy Macneill attended a family wedding, leaving him home to mind the three children. Never a fan of young people, Grandfather Macneill told the boys they could fight all night long if they wanted—and Well and Dave took him at his word.

They threw themselves into brawling with a delighted vengeance, while Maud and her cousin Clara sat calmly in the next room, a few yards apart from the din. The boys filled the kitchen with howls and thumps till ten that night, when Grandfather Macneill finally sent everybody to bed. The brothers were black-and-blue the next morning, but declared they'd had the time of their lives—and looked forward eagerly to the next family wedding.

The three children enjoyed calmer pleasures as well. They built a playhouse in a circle of spruces. The door was made of three rough boards with leather hinges cut from old boots, and the children planted a garden beside it. Their goals were ambitious: they sowed carrot seeds and parsnips, lettuce, beets, and flowers, but the only things that thrived, despite—or perhaps because of—all their feverish care were the wild, weedy live-forevers, and a few hardy sunflowers that lit the spruce grove with "cheery golden lamps."

Maud, Well, and Dave roamed through orchards and woods, played make-believe, picnicked out of doors, swung on homemade swings, built fires on cold winter nights. In the evenings they scared one another with ghost stories revolving around "the Haunted Wood"—a small grove of spruce set in the field just below the orchard.

They pretended to see mysterious "white things" flitting through the Haunted Wood, though they all had a fair suspicion that the ghosts were their own invention.

But one dim twilight Maud, Well, and Dave were playing in the grove when they all saw one of their dreaded *white things* creeping along the grass toward them. All three children saw the specter at the same instant. No doubt about it, this was real.

"Nonsense," Maud said, trying desperately to be practical and keep her head. It had to be the Macneills' white calf, she declared.

Well hurriedly agreed with Maud, but in truth, "the shapeless, groveling thing did not look in the least like a calf." Then it swiveled toward them.

"It's coming here!" Well shrieked, and the three children tore off to a neighbor's house, where the frightened servants armed themselves with pitchforks and buckets. No phantom immediately appeared—but a few minutes later Grandmother Macneill arrived with her knitting in one hand and in the other hand a long white tablecloth she'd left bleaching on the grass. She had flung it over her shoulder when the children began their stampede. The white cloth got caught over her head and she was trying to pull it loose as she stumbled along. The gruesome, lurching white thing was none other than Grandmother Macneill herself.

That July, in a storm, the cargo ship the *Marco Polo*

ran aground with its treasure and crew. All twenty members of the crew lodged in and around Cavendish. The staid village suddenly became a colorful place filled with noisy wagons of Irishmen, Spaniards, Norwegians, Dutchmen, Swedes, and—best of all to Maud, Well, and Dave—two Tahitians.

Since the Macneill home was one of the oldest in Cavendish, the *Marco Polo*'s captain boarded there—along with all the ship's gold. The Norwegian captain was an elderly gentleman, popular with his crew. His English was imperfect, but his manners were all one could wish. "Thank you for your kindness against me, little Miss Maud," he would chant with a deep bow.

One night the crew gathered in the front parlor for their pay. There, in the same room where Maud's young mother had lain in her coffin with her golden-brown hair spilling around her, the table stood heaped with sovereign coins. It was more gold than any of the children had ever seen. The lost treasure of her mother had been temporarily, magically transformed into piles of gold treasure.

Between ages seven and eleven, Maud thrived. She made good friends in school, and had the Nelson boys at home. It was the closest the young Maud came to a "normal" family life. The three children foraged for apples in season and went trout fishing in summer. One day in the nearby pond, Maud snagged a trout as large as any grown-up had ever caught, and Well and Dave looked at their friend with newfound respect. Maud was brave, resourceful, and willing. Together they followed the tracks of foxes and rabbits, picked berries, or trailed whistling robins into the woods.

Maud was a quick learner, lively and fun-loving, and despite her peculiar status as a semi-orphan, she became a leader among her schoolmates. She had a knack for inventing exciting things to do. Most of Maud's school friends were near or distant relatives, and they played in the woods behind the schoolhouse, along the seashore, and up and down Maud's favorite walk, a tree-filled haven she dubbed "Lover's Lane." The children played stepstone, Little Sally Water, blindman's buff, and drop-the-handkerchief. They coasted down the hill behind the schoolhouse in winter. One afternoon Maud and her chums led the whole school on a wild chase through fields, into woods and over muddy streams.

Then, just as suddenly as they'd appeared, one morning, Well and Dave Nelson vanished. There were no explanations, no discussions about where or why they went. Maud had no chance to say good-bye. Other living arrangements had been made for the boys. Their room was empty, every trace of their belongings removed. Perhaps the elder Macneills thought it kinder that way, or worried that Maud was getting too old to play with boys. Perhaps they failed to realize how much it would matter.

To Maud, the Nelson boys' sudden departure after

four years was as inexplicable and terrible as anything in a fairy tale. It would be decades before she laid eyes on Well and Dave again. The jolliest period of her childhood came to an abrupt end—but at age eleven Maud was on the verge of becoming a teenager, with piquant joys and trials ahead.

Alone once more, Maud turned back to her twin comforts: the worlds of nature and of books. And she had firmly in place her most enduring dream, the "one wish and ambition" of her childhood: to write, and to take her place among the world's "poets and artists and storytellers . . . who have never forgotten the way to fairyland."

CHAPTER FIVE

Room for Dreaming

Maud had one constant consolation all the time she was growing up in the Macneill homestead—the privacy of her own room. "A room where one sleeps and dreams and grieves and rejoices" takes on a life of its own, Maud wrote. Her summer suite of upstairs rooms became her essential and cherished place to dream and work.

Maud's grandparents sent their granddaughter to bed promptly at eight o'clock—but she didn't object, for her dream world began then, "that strange inner life of fancy which has always existed side by side with my outer life."

In winter the Macneills lived in the kitchen area, close

by the large cast-iron stove. It would have been too expensive to heat the whole house, so the family confined itself to the downstairs. Grandmother Macneill knitted or sewed, her work-worn hands always busy. Grandfather Macneill bent over the newspaper or sorted the mail. Sometimes on bitter nights, Grandmother and Grandfather Macneill slept in the warm kitchen. Maud stayed nearby, in her small, dim "winter bedroom," close to the hearth.

She desperately awaited spring and summer, when she could race back upstairs, "returned from exile . . . a queen in my own independent little kingdom." Her rooms overlooked a world of beauty: fields and woods and flowering fruit trees. She knelt by her casement window and over the low hills watched new moons "I shall remember in the halls of eternity."

As a young child, Maud slept in what was called the lookout, a tiny morsel of a room—basically, an oversized closet. Maud dubbed it her "boudoir," thinking it sounded elegant. Here she kept her first few books and magazines, her dolls, workbox, and treasured knickknacks. The view was of western Cavendish, over the trees of the garden to far hills and woods. "Poor little room!" she wrote in her journal. "I dreamed many a bright dream there." A few years later she moved into the larger den next door and her former boudoir became a trunk room.

Maud hung photographs, pictures, calendars, and

keepsakes, and kept the room well supplied with fresh blooms. Her bedspread was white, the wallpaper figured with small gay flowers. The room was open and airy; the only crowded space in it was her bookshelf.

On warm days Maud opened the casement window and listened to the singing of birds, the rustling of poplars. Even as a small girl, Maud's moods soared or plummeted according to the seasons. Her favorite time was late spring and early summer. Here was "a kingdom of beauty," she wrote. She delighted in summer rain pouring in green torrents over hills and fields. In fall she watched the flame of sunset, or the rising of a moon over the tip of a larch tree.

Each winter Maud returned to the dark downstairs "like a caged creature." The windows became so thickly covered with frost, she felt "literally imprisoned." One May evening she wrote, "I have moved upstairs again—which means that I have begun to live again. . . . To me it means the difference between happiness and unhappiness."

Of course, her summer den served an important function she never uttered aloud—it became her writer's study. Here Maud secretly composed her most beloved books: *Anne of Green Gables* and *Anne of Avonlea, Kilmeny of the Orchard* and *The Story Girl.*

The only view Maud lacked was east, facing the back orchard and the sea. It is exactly this east-facing view she gave to her most famous heroine, in the little "east room" of Green Gables. Everything in Maud's early life led to the writing of that book, but she had to overcome a hundred obstacles to achieve it.

At age nine, Maud presented her visiting father with her first poem, called "Autumn":

Now autumn comes, laden with peach and pear;
The sportsman's horn is heard throughout the land,
And the poor partridge, fluttering, falls dead.

What sort of poem is that? asked the bewildered Hugh John. Maud explained that it was blank verse. "Very blank," came the judgment. From that moment on, Maud's poems always rhymed. She also wrote all kinds of prose: "descriptions of my favourite haunts, biographies of my many cats, histories of visits, and school reviews."

Luckily for Maud, writing materials came readily and freely to hand. She began writing on the letterbills her frugal Grandfather Alexander Macneill saved from their home post office—unwanted scraps of colored paper used for post-office bills. A few years later, Maud wrote in the small yellow notebooks whose covers advertised patent medicines.

Maud's passionate fondness for books was considered odd at best, her dedication to writing dismissed as a flagrant waste of time. Maud hid her writings under the parlor sofa, on secret low shelves she had made by nailing two boards together.

The parlor was a refined hiding place. Maud considered it "the height of elegance," with its long lace curtains. The rug was "very gorgeous—all roses and ferns." To a more discerning eye, the elderly Macneills' decorations and furniture would have looked old-fashioned, presided over by a great black colonial mantelpiece out-of-date even in Maud's earliest childhood. Here in the least-used room of the house, tucked under the sofa, Maud secreted her earliest poems, stories, and diaries.

Though her grandparents considered writing a waste of time, Maud was surrounded all her life by storytellers. Her cantankerous Grandfather Macneill was a marvelous storyteller. So were her great-uncle Jimmie Macneill and great-aunt Mary Lawson. Mary, especially, was "a brilliant conversationalist . . . it was a treat to get Aunt Mary started on tales and recollections of her youth." Aunt Mary provided living proof that a woman could tell glorious stories and hold an audience captive. They were special chums, Mary Lawson and Maud—the elder woman in her seventies, Maud in her early teens. They exchanged confidences and tart opinions. "I cannot, in any words at my command, pay the debt I owe to Aunt Mary Lawson," Maud later declared.

At her one-room schoolhouse in Cavendish, Maud

formed a story club with friends. She specialized in melancholy tragedies. She wrote a long story called "My Graves" about a minister's wife who leaves a string of infant graves across the length and breadth of Canada. Maud also composed "The History of Flossy Brighteyes," about a doll who suffers every possible misfortune. "I couldn't kill a doll," she admitted, "but I dragged her through every other tribulation."

The year Maud turned twelve, the Cavendish school hired a new teacher—Miss Izzie Robinson. Izzie Robinson asked to board with the Macneills, as other teachers had done, but Grandfather Macneill put up a fight. He disliked female teachers—inside his house or out of them. Miss Robinson managed to foist herself on the Macneills as a boarder, but it led to such ugly quarrels that Maud had to withdraw from the Cavendish school for a time and attend a different school.

Maud hated being at the center of local gossip, as all of Cavendish followed the squabbling with interest. Grandfather was also feuding over some real or imagined slight with his eldest son, Maud's uncle John, who lived next door. Maud had always disliked this uncle. John Macneill was a forceful man who could be brutal when he didn't get his own way. He'd always frightened her. Maud did not like his sons any better, and felt miserable when she was forced to spend time in their company. The fighting both within the family and without put them all under a glaring spotlight.

Till Maud changed schools, Miss Robinson took her anger out on her young pupil—taunting and insulting Maud where she safely held the power. Maud hoped at least for a little praise for her writings, but none came from the immovable Miss Robinson. When Maud won honorable mention in the *Montreal Witness,* it was based on one of Alexander Macneill's favorite tales, which hardly endeared it to her teacher.

In desperation, Maud copied one of her own poems out as a song called "Evening Dreams" and asked Miss Robinson, a fine musician, if she knew it. Of course Miss Robinson did not—her own least-favorite student had written it.

The "song" began:

When the evening sun is setting
Quietly in the west,
In a halo of rainbow glory,
I sit me down to rest.

Miss Robinson declared it "very pretty," so Maud copied it over and sent it off with high hopes to an American magazine. It sailed back a few weeks later with her first— but not her last—rejection slip, and a note that she'd neglected to include a stamped return envelope. Maud next tried the local paper, which promptly rejected it. It was years before she even attempted to publish again.

Maud destroyed her early works one by one. Later she wished she had those first efforts back—even the melancholy "My Graves" and "The History of Flossie Brighteyes." When Maud was fourteen she read over her old childhood diaries and burned those, too—to her everlasting regret.

A few months short of her fifteenth birthday, Maud began "a new kind of diary." She declared the old writing so silly that she was ashamed of it. With characteristic self-mockery, she noted that she had written in it "religiously every day and told what kind of weather it was." She would have thought it "a kind of crime" not to write in it every single day—"nearly as bad as not saying my prayers, or washing my face."

In her new journal she determined to write "only when I have something worth writing about. Life is beginning to get interesting for me—I will soon be fifteen." She was not going to record so much about the weather, she vowed. And, she added emphatically, "last but not least—I am going to keep this book locked up!!"

By now Maud had won a few composition awards. These early victories heartened her. Best of all, Cavendish had hired a new schoolteacher, Miss Hattie Gordon, who encouraged Maud's literary efforts. In fact, she insisted all the schoolchildren write compositions every week.

The labor of writing was play to Maud. When she was "scribbling," time flew by. "Oh, as long as we can work we can make life beautiful!" she exclaimed.

Maud gratefully returned to her seat beside her beloved Amanda Macneill ("Mollie") and other classmates. Miss Gordon expected fine things of all her students. She encouraged them in musical events, nature outings, and recitations, and organized school picnics at the end of each year. "I like her splendidly," Maud enthused in her diary.

Miss Gordon was not conventionally pretty, but her looks were striking; she was "a true lady," with a lovely smile and fair wavy hair. She was quick-tempered but seldom gave in to it, going silent till her anger passed. Maud revered her for being the sort of teacher who "had the power of inspiring a love of study for its own sake."

Miss Gordon participated in the Cavendish Literary Society—and encouraged her students to do the same. This was just the support that Maud had been needing. The Macneills had banned Maud from "the Literary," dismissing it as a waste of time, thus keeping Maud from the only resource that could feed her hunger for books and literary talk. But if all the other children were participating, Maud could hardly be the only pupil kept home. So Maud was at last allowed to join the longed-for Literary—and to recite in public.

Maud took as her first recital piece "The Child

Martyr." She recited with "flashing eyes and fervently clasped hands," a neighbor reported. If anyone wanted to know what Anne of Green Gables really looked like, he declared, they need only have observed Maud in her trembling excitement. She was finally part of the literary life, an introduction that opened the way to new possibilities, new books—and her first romance.

CHAPTER SIX

Count Nine Stars

Some folks declared Maud was "boy crazy"; she attracted the boys with her quick wit and vivacity. Uncle John's daughter, Lucy, living right next door, probably told unkind tales against her popular cousin. Her strict grandparents kept a tighter rein on Maud than ever. Any time Maud left the house for a walk in her beloved Lover's Lane, she was closely questioned. Even a simple walk by the shore would provoke an inquisition.

But Maud did have two female friends who were approved by her grandparents. One was Amanda Macneill, her old buddy "Mollie." The other was Penzie Macneill, a cousin a few years older. In typical schoolgirl "crushes" of the time, Maud and Penzie exchanged sentimental poems and letters, declaring their mutual devotion.

Maud and Mollie had their two favorite boys at school, whom they nicknamed "Snip" and "Snap." Snip was Nathan Lockhart, a slim, bright-eyed, fatherless boy, and the cleverest boy in school. Nate was crazy about books and writing. He was allowed to join the Literary before Maud won permission, and would sneak her a few treasured books to borrow. Snap was Nate's best friend, John Laird—a handsome, good-natured fellow. In their early teens, Mollie-and-Polly and Snip-and-Snap became an inseparable foursome. They led their friends and classmates in popularity and in academics, and Maud and Nathan Lockhart formed a friendly rivalry over who placed first in school.

Nate's father had drowned at sea before Nate was born. Nate, like Maud, understood about early loss. His pastor uncle, Arthur John Lockhart, was a respected poet, which gave Nate further standing in Maud's eyes. She stayed friends with "Pastor Felix" all her life, and dedicated one of her finest novels, *Emily Climbs,* to him. When Maud placed third in a school essay contest, Nate bested her by placing second. Unlike the fictional Anne, Maud proved a gracious rival. "It is better than mine," she admitted.

Though Maud claimed no romantic interest in Nate Lockhart, they were close comrades; they teased, argued, made up, and supported each other. Her teenage journal entries rise and fall depending on whether she and Snip are getting along or having one of their frequent misunderstandings. In her diary she wrote, "Snip is a very nice boy and we are great friends. He is crazy about books and so am I. . . . And the other scholars don't like it because we talk of things they don't understand."

In November 1889, a few weeks shy of Maud's fifteenth birthday, Maud and Mollie were walking home from a religious lecture in the cold and dark when Snip decided to escort them home. This was a great event in a young woman's life—the first night she walked home holding a young man's arm. Maud declared she felt "silly," but she and Mollie stayed up all night talking about it.

Alas, they weren't the only ones talking. Another pair of girls happened to see Nate accompanying Maud home. Word traveled fast in Cavendish. By the next day, the whole school knew.

A few weeks later Maud, Mollie, and Nate enjoyed another "scrumptious walk home." This led to worse gossip, which turned into a months-long series of spats among the schoolgirls. Rumors and accusations flew thick and fast, leaving Maud and Mollie and their innocent escapades far behind. Finally, an exasperated Miss Hattie Gordon sat all the girls down and got things sorted out. To Maud's credit, she had no interest in fighting or gossip, and she valued her reputation as honest and straightforward. Nor did she want to risk her newfound freedom to attend social events like the Literary.

Maud had begun to look like a young lady. Her hair had been golden blond as a child but had darkened, first to the color of autumn leaves, then to nearly brunette. Her eyes were unusual, the pupils so large "that her eyes appeared black instead of blue or gray."

All this time Maud described Nate as only a "good chum," but she felt desolate whenever they quarreled. "Oh dear. I feel glum. I know Nate is mad at me." She never meant to vex him, but she wrote in her journal, "I am a horrid little goose, I know," and worse, "I can't help being a horrid little goose." A few days later she would report that she and Nate were good friends again. He was certainly a "nice boy," she stoutly maintained, "clever and intellectual, and that is more than can be said" of the others.

Maud had always been an outsider in Cavendish, but she grew more aware of the division between her inner and outer life in her teenage years. There was no place where she could be whole. Maud constructed a separate inward existence "very different indeed from the world in which I lived, moved, and had my outward being." One Maud went to school, diligently did her homework, attended church, and kept her mouth shut. The other sported with otherworldly beings, ruled imaginary kingdoms, fought demons. These real and imaginative worlds "clashed hopelessly and irreconcilably," and she learned to keep them separate—at a cost.

Her relatives accused Maud of being "deep" and "sly." Cousin Lucy's gossip hadn't helped matters. In one of Maud's Emily novels, her heroine wonders why she would be thought sly. "I think it is because I have a habit when I am bored or disgusted with people, of stepping suddenly into my own world and shutting the door."

Nate Lockhart was Maud's closest intellectual companion. In her journal, Maud wrote, "It was so dreadfully lonesome the last time we quarreled." Nate often came along on long rambles with Maud and Mollie. Together they'd attend debates and lectures, or coast downhill on sleds—there was safety and comfort in the threesome. "We talked of many things we three, soberly but not sadly," wrote Maud in her journal. "We were all too happy for sadness."

The year Maud turned fifteen, the Cavendish school got caught up in a new romantic craze. First, a boy or girl had to count nine stars for nine nights in a row. The first person you shook hands with next would be your true love.

On February 17, 1890, Nate Lockhart counted his ninth star and shook hands with a girl—but he refused to name her, even to Mollie and Maud. Maud finally wheedled the answer out of him by agreeing to answer "fair and square, without any evasion, any one question he might ask me."

Nate summoned up his courage and asked, "Which of your boy friends do you like best?"

Maud wrote, rather snippily: "You have a little more brains than the other Cavendish boys and I like brains—so I suppose I like you best—though I don't see why I should, after the trick you have played on me."

Nate handed Maud the following note the next day at school, February 18, 1890, which she copied into her journal:

I have altered my plan of arrangement and resolved to give you hard, dry, plain facts, for they may possibly appear as such to you, but they are nevertheless as true as gospel. Here goes—Of all my feminine friends the one whom I most admire—no, I'm growing reckless—the one whom I love . . . is L. M. Montgomery, the girl I shook hands with, the girl after my own heart.

It's hard not to admire the young man who wrote that brave note and reached out for that "heart-hungry" girl. Nate Lockhart seems a likely early model for the famous Gilbert Blythe, whom Anne Shirley marries and loves truly for the rest of her life. Like Gilbert, Nate was a worthy rival, a true friend, a fellow intellect, and a steady, loving personality. Photos reveal a thin, handsome boy with fair wavy hair, large ears, and an intense, level gaze. He has a strong jawline and firm mouth, indicating his own degree of stubbornness. Other girls were "crazy" about Nate. And he, apparently, was crazy about Maud.

But Maud's response was mixed. On one hand she wrote in her journal in exultation, "he not only liked me best—he loved me!" Maud had feared he might name some other girl and was ready to change her own letter in an instant and write in the name of Snap instead—Nate's friend John Laird. Maud felt a flash of joy, "a queer, foolish, triumphant little feeling about it." She had grown so unsure of her lovability that she had often wondered if "anyone would ever care for me—that way." Now she knew, without any doubt, that someone could and did.

Yet she also felt like a "perfect idiot," and the next time Maud was alone with Nate, she felt "rather frightened and silly." Nate was wise enough not to push the matter—but he did give Maud another letter, now lost to history. All we know is that she wasn't sure "whether I liked it or not." In some ways, she wrote, she did, "and in others I didn't."

Maud managed to evade Nate for the rest of the school year and kept him safely surrounded by plenty of other "chums." They took part in various scrapes and school events—one spring day scrubbing down the whole school, nearly blowing up the old school stove in the process. The young folks held mayflower picnics and conducted the final school concert of the year, declared "a great success." But Maud avoided spending time alone with Nate, fearful of what romantic thing he might say or do next. Years later she wrote that she simply had not been attracted to him and that their match would have been a disaster. "Why is it," she asked plaintively, "that all through my life the men I've *liked* best were the ones I couldn't *love*?"

It is perhaps the central question of Maud's personal life. She was a terrible judge of the opposite sex. She loved the wrong men, always. Maud believed that friendship was based on similarities between people, and that passionate love was based on difference. Had Nate been less familiar, less like Maud herself, she might not have dismissed him so easily.

That spring, Maud offered friendship instead of her love, and Nate accepted. But he kept trying to court Maud when school was out for the year. It was no use; Maud was confident of her own inclinations.

Most of the marriages Maud observed firsthand were uneven partnerships. Grandmother Lucy Macneill managed her cantankerous husband by surrendering her will to his, maintaining independence in the domestic arena, resorting to subterfuge when necessary. Their marriage would hardly have inspired young Maud to seek out a partner of her own.

When Nate Lockhart declared his love, he and Maud were only fifteen years old. Maud was too young and ambitious to consider a serious courtship. Had they both stayed on in Cavendish, something might have blossomed between them, for Nate Lockhart was every bit as determined as Maud. Instead, an irresistible, unexpected invitation that summer swept Maud far from Nate Lockhart and everything she called home. It would have taken more than nine stars for Maud to have resisted its call.

CHAPTER SEVEN

"Darling Father" and Prince Albert

In April of 1890, the fifteen-year-old Maud learned that her father, Hugh John, was thinking about inviting her to join him out in Western Canada. Hugh John Montgomery had remarried, started a new family, and was beginning to ease into the business of land settlement and real estate. He thought of making the family whole again. Maud dared not believe it at first. "I am frightened to think or say much about it," she confided to her diary.

But by August, it had become a definite plan, with her grandfather Senator Donald Montgomery escorting Maud on the long train journey west to Saskatchewan. The cautious Macneills agreed that Maud might stay on for a year or more, only after repeated assurance that Maud would receive just as good an education as she could find in Cavendish.

Hugh John had proven he could support a wife and family. Maud longed to be with her "darling father" again. The teenager had begun to rebel in earnest against the restrictions set by her strict grandparents. They never approved, she fumed, "of anything which means the assembling of the young folks together."

Maud and her thorny Grandfather Macneill never had an easygoing relationship, but now they constantly butted heads, and Grandmother Lucy Macneill could not always reconcile the arguments between them. With both apprehension and relief, the elderly couple allowed their lively teenage granddaughter to rejoin her father out west.

Maud was all optimistic effervescence about the move. Maud had been waiting all her life for someone to call "mother," and she was fully prepared to love her new stepmother. She felt thrilled to travel to new places and, of course, to be reunited with her Papa. Only on the eve of leaving Cavendish did she allow herself a few doubts. Would she like remote Prince Albert? And could she love her new stepmother, "just as if she were really my mother"?

Maud set out with high hopes on her journey on August 9, 1890. This time she did not stay with her "merry cousins" at Park Corner, but at the impressive home of her paternal grandfather, the Senator. He looked like a figure out of a storybook. Grandfather Montgomery was handsome, kindly, jolly, and outgoing. He "fed her up" as best he could, convinced that his slender granddaughter was "hollow all the way down" to her boots.

As a grand surprise, he introduced Maud to the premier of Canada, Sir John A. MacDonald, and his stately wife. This was heady stuff for a fifteen-year-old girl from tiny Cavendish. But Maud kept her wits about her. Sir John, she declared in her diary, was "not handsome but pleasant-faced." His wife was impressive but homely, and worse still, in Maud's eyes, dressed "very dowdily."

Prince Albert constituted the farthest reaches of the newly federated nation of Canada, and to reach it, Maud and her grandfather had to endure ferries and trains, long carriage drives and still more trains. Many passages were steep and dangerous. Sometimes the train slowed to a crawl, or stopped when a cow wandered onto the tracks. They passed through "the wooded hills of Maine," through Montreal, past the bleak northern wilds of Ontario. Maud kept her trusty notebook by her side and sat glued to the train window. Montreal, she declared, was a fine city—but she would never want to live there. She was not a city girl. Every shoreline enchanted her and reminded her of home.

Grandfather Montgomery tried to provide company on their long journey west, but he was quite deaf — and trains in those days were noisy, dusty affairs. Conversation was impossible. Maud stayed in her tiny sleeping berth — so cramped that she kept sitting up too quickly and banging her head on the ceiling. The one place she could safely venture on her own was the balcony of the Ladies' Parlor, where she could only sit and wait and hope to be addressed. One old lady plied her with questions — till she discovered Maud was Presbyterian. Hearing this, she fled without another word. Another "Yankee" lady, who seemed at first severe and silent, turned out to be friendly and companionable. Maud was sorry to see her depart on the Halifax train.

When they stopped at a city, Grandfather Montgomery would disappear for hours, leaving Maud to fend for herself. She'd steel herself to disembark and walk around the train depot — usually on the outskirts of town, as in Winnipeg, which, she wrote, looked as if someone had tossed out a handful of houses and streets "and forgotten to sort them out afterwards." But then, she consoled herself, the real town might be a good deal more promising — if only she could get anywhere near it.

On August 18, 1890, after more than a week of grueling travel, Maud and Grandfather Montgomery pulled into the western town of Regina. There, a marvelous surprise awaited them. Grandfather left to check for the mail. He came back a little while later declaring that he had a special friend who wanted to see Maud. She opened her door and nearly fell into the arms of her father.

Maud had not laid eyes on Hugh John in five years. He had not changed from the merry, openhearted man she'd adored. Father and daughter laughed and cried for joy. That instant of reunion made the whole arduous journey worthwhile. Hugh John arranged to drive them around Regina — a barren place in those days — but Maud couldn't take her eyes off her father.

The next day they set off by caboose and then buckboard for Prince Albert. The countryside was covered with gay blue wildflowers. Prince Albert was less than thirty years old, barely more than a settlement along the riverbank. It was too new for its own train station. In 1890, the year Maud arrived, Prince Albert had a population of a little over one thousand, in addition to the Indian settlement to the west. Where everything back home in Cavendish was familiar and filtered through hundreds of years of history, Prince Albert was true pioneer country — raw and untested.

Hugh John had given his modest new house the lofty name Eglintoun Villa in honor of the family's supposed connection to the Scottish earls of Eglinton. Hugh John had met and married his boss's stepdaughter, Mary Ann McRae, niece of a railway millionaire. They had lived exiled in Battleford for three years before moving back to Eglintoun Villa with their growing family. It was to Eglintoun Villa, her new house of dreams, that Maud came with such high hopes that August afternoon.

Maud met her new "Mamma" and her two-and-a-half-year-old half sister, Kate, "a very pretty child." The newest member of the household was Edith Skelton, or Edie, a girl Maud's age responsible for helping Mary Ann Montgomery with household chores.

Maud quickly became friends with Edie—and just as quickly grew to dislike her twenty-seven-year-old stepmother. Maud had been brought west to serve as a mother's helper and unpaid nanny—treated more like a servant than a family member. The name "Mamma" quickly fell by the wayside, though Maud used it to please her father around company. Otherwise Mary Ann Montgomery was simply "Mrs. Montgomery" to her stepdaughter.

Hugh John earned too little to please his ambitious young wife. He worked numerous jobs at once, as homestead assessor, auctioneer, real estate salesman, and inspector for the local railroad. The Senator had already helped financially and in locating employment for his son out west. Now Hugh John was on his own. Mary Ann

Montgomery had grown up in wealth and comfort. She nagged her husband to earn more and mocked him for his dreams of grandeur. With one small child at home and pregnant again, Mary Ann resented Maud's presence in the house. She told Hugh John that his pet names for his older daughter were "babyish" and wouldn't let him use them. She begrudged any time that father and daughter spent alone together. She was determined never to wait on Maud, refusing even to pour her a cup of tea at mealtime.

Maud had come hoping to be welcomed as a daughter. Instead she became a Cinderella figure in her father's home. Maud shared a small room with Edie. When Mrs. Montgomery left the house, she locked up the pantry. Mary Ann spent days at a time not speaking to Maud at all. She forbade the five-foot-five-inch Maud to wear her hair up, for fear that an older daughter would make her look old. Maud felt desperately homesick. It was only her hopes of a good education, and the sight of her father looking at her with eyes that "just shine with love" that kept her in Prince Albert.

Maud and Edie attended the same small free public high school in town. There were only nine pupils, six boys and three girls, including Mrs. Montgomery's half sister, Annie McTaggart. The young teacher, John Mustard ("What a funny name!" Maud exclaimed in her diary), was a former school friend of Mrs. Montgomery's. John Mustard was well educated and ambitious, studying to become a minister.

The old Prince Albert schoolhouse had burned down, so Maud and her schoolmates had their classes in the town hall, formerly a hotel. Their tiny classroom doubled as a ladies' dressing room on ball nights, and students would find hairpins, feathers, flowers, and an occasional broken hand mirror on the floor the next morning. The police headquarters and town jail were located there in the schoolhouse. Petty criminals and drunks were locked up right behind their classroom. Maud once went exploring and accidentally locked herself into a jail cell.

Maud disliked her new schoolmaster, Mr. Mustard, though he was strikingly handsome — fair-haired and tall, with blue eyes and a "golden moustache which he cultivates very carefully." But she did not believe he would make "a very brilliant preacher." The teacher's long-standing friendship with her stepmother didn't improve Maud's opinion of him. John Mustard was intelligent, but he taught stiffly, by rote, without the energy Maud was used to from Miss Gordon. He was authoritarian, and did not hesitate to use a leather whip on boys who misbehaved.

Maud decided to earn her teacher's degree, adding to her coursework. Maud liked going to school, especially as more students arrived. Earning a teaching degree would give her credentials she could use in the future. And Grandfather Macneill was not there to oppose her plans.

By October, young Edie had fled the Montgomery household. Mrs. Montgomery had pressed Edie to spy on Maud, though the loyal Edie resisted. Hugh John was always away on business, trying to earn money every way possible. More and more household duties fell upon Maud, and her relationship with her stepmother unraveled. Mrs. Montgomery opened and read Maud's letters from home and would certainly have read Maud's journal had she not kept it carefully locked and hidden away.

Winter brought record-breaking cold to Prince Albert, with temperatures plummeting many degrees below zero. It also brought an unexpected gentleman caller to the Montgomery household — the schoolmaster himself, John Mustard.

Maud's father was out that first evening, so Maud ran to tell her stepmother John Mustard was there, only to find that Mrs. Montgomery had mysteriously jumped into bed, clothes and all, and refused to come downstairs. Mary Ann Montgomery clearly believed she'd found a good match for her stepdaughter and was doing her best to move things along. So Maud was left to entertain Mr. Mustard for the evening — the first of many long evenings to follow.

Maud was clever and vivacious, a good student, and,

John Mustard had obviously decided, a likely prospect for a minister's wife. He did not take any of Maud's hints that she disagreed. He couldn't be put off by her coolness, even when it bordered on outright rudeness. He went on calling night after night, while Mrs. Montgomery kept herself conveniently out of sight.

By day in the classroom John Mustard was often low-spirited or sulky for no apparent reason. But back he would come again, each week, hat in hand. "And he is such a bore!" Maud fumed. All winter and spring, Mr. Mustard continued his unwelcome calls. She found the courtship unbearable. Even Maud's father joined in the teasing, grinning each time he asked her at the dinner table to pass him the *mustard*.

That spring, Maud made two treasured new friends: a brother and sister named Will and Laura Pritchard. Like most girls in town, Laura attended the local private convent school—but Mrs. Montgomery was not about to spend good money on Maud when a free education was available. The friends found ways to be together after school. Laura and Maud could talk happily for hours on any and every subject imaginable. "We are twin spirits in every way," Maud declared.

Laura's brother Will was Maud's favorite classmate. He had red hair, bright green eyes, and a mischievous, crooked smile. He brought liveliness and high spirits into their dull classroom. The day he arrived, sitting in the row behind

Maud, he told her he couldn't concentrate with her beautiful hair right in front of him. He had a natural warmth that enchanted Maud, and soon he and Maud were cracking jokes, passing notes — and driving poor Mr. Mustard crazy. The threesome went out for long moonlight rides, joking, talking, stargazing. Here for the first time ever in her life, Maud declared that she had found her true "kindred spirits."

That winter there was one more glory to come. Maud had never forgotten her grandfather's favorite tale, an exciting one about Cape LeForce. She'd composed a new poem about it and sent it off to the *Charlottetown Patriot*. Maud's father presented her with a copy of the newspaper when it arrived by mail. Right there in print, for all the world to see, was Maud's own poem! The paper shook in her hands; the letters of her name danced in front of her eyes. Here at last was a real, true publication.

Maud called it "the proudest day" of her life. Hugh John was openly delighted; he praised Maud to the skies, while his wife merely glanced at the paper and refused to utter a word of congratulations.

That winter, with the new baby due any time, Hugh John made a sudden turn toward politics. His luck and timing were poor, as always. He shifted his alliance from his father's Conservative party to the Liberal ticket — and promptly lost his bid for parliament.

In February, Mary Ann gave birth to a son named

Donald Bruce. She hired a girl to replace Edie and gave her Maud's own treasured "Southview" room. But the new girl lasted only a few days. She declared that Mrs. Montgomery was "too cross and particular" to bear. Mary Ann didn't even pretend to look for new hired help. Instead she put Maud to work. The new baby was colicky; nerves were strained. Mary Ann used her energy to care for her two children. All the rest of the household drudgery fell upon Maud.

It was impossible for Maud to keep up with all the chores and do schoolwork, too. The choice was clear. Maud had to drop out of the Prince Albert school altogether. She held up as best she could and refused to complain, "because it would make father feel so bad." But the teenager began to suffer from headaches that would plague her the rest of her life.

Maud confided her troubles only to her journal. Writing was her one escape. She kept on composing poems, stories, and articles as well writing in her diary. The poem printed in the Charlottetown paper had given her hope. She diligently practiced the "art she worshipped." She later wrote of this period that the "flame of an ambition to write something big was beginning to sear my soul." Her essay was published in the *Prince Albert Times* and *Saskatchewan Review* and reprinted in the Winnipeg papers. Another story won a prize competition and appeared in the *Montreal Witness*.

Her father sang Maud's praises to anyone who would listen. Her stepmother pointedly ignored each new success. But Maud was sixteen now, and determined. Years earlier she had clipped from a magazine a poem called "The Fringed Gentian" and pasted it into her writing portfolio. She quoted it in her *Emily* books, and later it was used as the title for her reissued memoir, *The Alpine Path*. She clung to those verses as a teenager doing backbreaking, thankless household work thousands of miles from home.

Then whisper, blossom, in thy sleep
How I may upward climb
The Alpine path, so hard, so steep,
That leads to heights sublime?
How I may reach the far-off goal
Of true and honored fame,
To write upon its shining scroll
A woman's humble name.

Though Maud no longer could attend school, she still enjoyed church events and Sunday school, and took part in school recitals, where her gifts won special praise in the local paper. Her father stayed away more often than ever, and Mary Ann Montgomery was harried and distracted. Once Maud's chores were done, there was no one to supervise her. For the first time, she conducted a social life unchaperoned—attending tobogganing parties, picnics, and excursions, even dances in the nearby army barracks. The elderly Macneills would have been horrified—but of course Maud did not report to them.

Maud felt terribly homesick, despite the social whirl. She wrote to her friend Penzie that the day she would return to Cavendish "will be the happiest one of my life." She had traveled to Prince Albert in high hopes of getting a fine education and obtaining a teaching degree—and all that had fallen away. Even her coveted independence turned stale. Like a child who can finally eat all the junk food she likes, Maud found her new freedom lacked nourishment. No one watched over her, no one put her well-being first. Her only true friends were Will and Laura Pritchard, but both attended school during the day.

John Mustard kept calling on Maud in the evenings, sometimes as often as three times a week, though she offered no encouragement. By now his romantic intentions were unmistakable, even to Maud, who had a gift for ignoring the obvious. She found her suitor interesting only when he talked about theology—but on nearly every other subject he was deadly tedious. She resented her stepmother's assumption that John Mustard was a great catch. Maud wanted more than security; she craved a kindred spirit. She was barely civil to John Mustard's face and mocked him cruelly in her journals.

John Mustard was to prove himself a loyal friend to Maud all her life. He was an intelligent young man with a fine future ahead. He became a popular and highly respected minister, despite Maud's dismissal. "Hate is only love that has missed its way," Maud once wrote. She would come to regret her teenage rudeness, and puzzle over John Mustard's early devotion to a hopeless cause.

The poor man finally gathered his courage and asked Maud if she could see their friendship growing into something else.

"I don't see what it *can* develop into, Mr. Mustard," she replied coolly.

There were tears in his eyes, but none in Maud's. She was relieved that the long, futile courtship was over. "I never could understand why John Mustard endured it. I was a pretty girl, but I was never such a distracting beauty that a man would be involved in such an infatuation. . . . Yet he kept up the crazy pursuit until he had to be flatly refused. . . . I have always felt queerly ashamed of the whole incident."

By spring, it was agreed that Maud would return home to Cavendish. Her stepmother was glad to get rid of her sulky teenage stepdaughter. Mary Ann didn't even come to the station to say good-bye. Her father, that gentlest of men, may have been relieved to see an end to the squabbles—for if Maud refused to complain,

Mary Ann Montgomery felt no such compunction.

Maud felt very differently saying good-bye to the charming, green-eyed Will Pritchard than to John Mustard. Maud described Will as "the nicest boy" she'd ever known. She would not admit even to herself how strongly she felt. If Maud was lying to herself, she did it convincingly — she was, after all, a budding young fiction writer. "He just seems like a brother or a jolly good comrade," she insisted in her journal.

But in Maud's last few days in Prince Albert, she was anxiously waiting for something. Time was running out. Will Pritchard always said "pretty things" to her, but nothing as definite as John Mustard. Laura Pritchard assured Maud that Will would be brokenhearted after she left. She told Maud, "I know this — he just worships the ground you tread on." Will asked for Maud's photograph, for a lock of her hair, and he coaxed from her finger a little gold ring that she always wore — "but then," Maud admitted, "he didn't have to coax very hard."

Their final farewell was sad, "dream-like," and rather formal. He was going away on a short trip the next day. Will held out a hand to say good-bye and said to "have a very happy time — and don't forget me." He gave Maud a sealed going-away letter. Then they shook hands and parted.

That night, Maud opened Will's letter. In it he confessed that he loved her — but he had already left town.

If he hadn't been so far away, Maud confessed, she might have run after him. Instead she boarded the train for home the next morning.

It was unthinkable in those days for a young woman to make such a long, harrowing journey alone. Yet that is just what Maud did. She had no other option. The solitary teenager passed through endless miles of dull prairie landscape, crowded upright, crammed three-in-a-row into train seats meant to accommodate two. She catnapped as best she could. Maud had to change trains several times, find her own overnight accommodations in strange cities, and walk through rough city streets unescorted. She boarded over noisy saloons. Her solitude made her an easy target for thieves and worse. She was sixteen, slender, and shapely, no longer a child. Mary Rubio, one of the great authorities on the life and work of L. M. Montgomery, writes flatly, "No decent father would have allowed his sixteen-year-old daughter to make such a trip alone."

Maud met the challenge head-on and with her eyes open. She admired the countryside, relished the spray off the Great Lakes, and spent her Sunday night in a saloon, jotting notes under a brilliant electric light with the din of the bar crowd around her. In Toronto, Maud called on family friends only to find they were not home — so she spent five hours sociably chatting with the governess and children.

Her train arrived in Ottawa at five a.m., but

Grandfather Montgomery, who was scheduled to meet her, had overslept. He finally caught up with her "in a great flurry . . . bless his dear heart." Maud had hoped to spend some more time with him, but he quickly sent her home to Prince Edward Island, now with a proper chaperone.

When Maud arrived at Prince Edward Island on September 5, 1891, there was no one at the station to meet her. She sat for two hours alone in the waiting room at Summerside, then took another train to Kensington. Still nobody came. "It did seem a chilly home-coming," she admitted. Undaunted, she hired a wagon team to take her to Park Corner, where Aunt Annie, Uncle John, and her cousins greeted her joyfully. She stayed on a few more days, still hoping for some word of welcome and invitation from her own grandparents in Cavendish.

None came. Maud waited. And waited. Maud's uncle Crosby—a Park Corner relative—finally took pity on her and drove her back to Cavendish. Maud perked up as soon as she began to see familiar landmarks. She nearly fell out of the cart, wild with excitement, by the time she caught a glimpse of home. Poor Uncle Crosby, she decided, "must have thought he had a crazy girl on his hands."

"Do not imagine that places don't love us back," she once wrote. Maud might have been cautious with suitors, but the trees, ponds, red clay, and blue waters of Prince Edward Island she loved passionately, without reservation.

The dream of a home life with her father was now forever at an end. She must build her own new house of dreams.

CHAPTER EIGHT

The Pill inside the Jam

Maud arrived in Cavendish only to find Grandfather Macneill more peevish and opposed to all her plans than ever. He hoped his granddaughter would stay home and behave. Both grandparents expected her to settle down into learning more housewifely arts — at which, in fact, Maud excelled. She skillfully quilted, sewed, embroidered, and baked. But the Macneills could not have been more wrong about their granddaughter's goals and ambitions.

The first place Maud visited on her return was her old one-room schoolhouse. She spotted the nail where she'd always hung her hat; above that nail, Nate had carved her name in a special cipher. Here were the old desks where she'd sat with her friends; there, the worn wood door and carved initials of now-defunct couples. At first glance, the old school seemed unchanged. The next day, a Saturday, she and Mollie went back together—pushing up a window to climb in.

They found the place sadly abandoned, with its rows of empty chairs. Maud and Mollie climbed out again and crept to the nearby wood, half-expecting Nate Lockhart and Jack Laird to come along, listening for the sound of their familiar whistle. But Nate was off at Arcadia College; Jack already teaching school. Only a year had passed, but to Maud it seemed "ages" had gone by.

While all her schoolmates had moved forward, Maud had fallen sadly behind. She'd lost a valuable year in Prince Albert. College was farther from her grasp than ever. "If I could only manage to get a little more education!" she fumed. That dream at the moment seemed "impossible." The Macneills had no intention of supporting Maud in a college education—even if they'd had the easy means to do so, or had she acquired the needed academic preparation.

Miss Gordon remained one of Maud's few supporters. She organized one of her elaborate school concerts that fall and encouraged Maud and other former students to lend a hand. Maud threw herself into the preparations—helping to decorate the hall, cleaning, arranging seats, delivering dramatic dialogues that "brought down the house."

With Miss Gordon's encouragement, Maud set herself a course of independent study that winter, anxious to make up lost ground. She studied English history, physical geography, Latin, geometry, and English literature. All this study kept Maud from feeling lonely and lost. The sheer volume of her writing output in these early years was impressive: stories, poems, and essays. She had her old pals Mollie, Penzie, and others for company. She attended the Cavendish Literary Society. And she woke early and stayed up late to study alone.

Grandmother Macneill, at least, must have taken notice. That February, Lucy Macneill did something strikingly out of character. Ever a creature of habit and isolation, she suddenly took it into her head to visit her relatives at Park Corner—unaccompanied.

No one knows exactly what Grandmother Macneill said or did there. But when she came home, it had somehow been arranged that sixteen-year-old Maud would live at Park Corner for a few months, giving music lessons to her cousins there. And . . . miracle of miracles, she would be *paid* for her teaching.

Aunt Annie and Uncle John had never expressed any interest in music lessons before—a luxury they could scarcely afford. But Grandmother Macneill had a little independent money. She'd earned it by doing extra work at the homestead, and by taking in boarders. In all likelihood, she herself paid Maud's salary. It would help to keep her granddaughter occupied in a more sociable house. It was also a way to sneak some education money into Maud's pocket without Grandfather Macneill realizing it.

Maud spent three happy months at Aunt Annie and Uncle John's. There were sleigh rides, family parties, and weddings. Park Corner buzzed with life and activity. Other relatives lived nearby, including Maud's handsome and clever cousin, Edwin Simpson.

Maud's literary prospects took a turn for the better, too. She had begun publishing children's stories in Sunday-school magazines, heavy on preachy endings. Her favorite kind of story for young readers, she declared, was "a good jolly one" without a hidden sermon stuck inside it "like a pill in a spoonful of jam." But at least this treacly work was getting published and noticed. The lieutenant governor of the Northwest Territories praised Maud to Grandpa Montgomery, asking for her photograph and for copies of other stories she had written.

Will Pritchard was now only a pen pal living thousands of miles away. When Nate Lockhart came home to visit, he loftily informed Maud she had "a fair intellect" and might make something of herself someday—if she could go to college. Maud continued to write, to dream, and to hope. But the world was moving on without her. Even ever-faithful Miss Gordon left Cavendish for Oregon. Maud felt the loss keenly. She had lost "a true friend," she wrote sadly, the last in Cavendish "who sympathized with me in my ambitions and efforts."

As it turned out, Maud was wrong. She still had one significant ally: Grandmother Lucy Macneill. Maud had earned a little money giving music lessons at Park Corner, but not enough to pay for college. She had set her sights on Prince of Wales College in nearby Charlottetown — the nearest and least expensive place to earn her teacher's certificate. Even this modest goal remained hopelessly out of reach.

That fall, without telling anyone about it, Lucy Macneill wrote to her former son-in-law, Hugh John, begging him to contribute something, anything at all, toward his daughter's education. When he failed to respond, Lucy made up the difference herself, paying the money out of her own meager household account. It was a great personal and financial sacrifice. With this unexpected windfall, Maud's dream of attending Prince of Wales College came within her grasp. It was to be, as she later declared, "the happiest year" of her life.

CHAPTER NINE

The Happiest Year

Once Maud had gained Grandmother Macneill's financial support, all that was needed was hard work—and that had never kept Maud from anything. She returned to school and readied herself for the difficult entrance exam to Prince of Wales College. She missed her "old crowd" but part of her thrilled just to be back in a classroom again. She sat in her former seat with the view of spruce woods, and went for long walks alone during recess. She studied with a vengeance, read every book she could lay her hands on. Once she teased a red-haired boy classmate who would not speak to her again for months. That episode made its way into *Anne of Green Gables*—but in her novel it was redheaded Anne who held the grudge.

Maud grew fond of the young new Cavendish school-teacher, Miss Selena Robinson. They worked hard preparing Maud for college, and by June the young scholar was bubbling over with anticipation. Just one hurdle lay ahead—the dreaded entrance exams. Maud was tantalizingly close to what had seemed a hopeless fantasy—the dream of "a little more education."

In July 1893, eighteen-year-old Maud headed off to Charlottetown, full of excitement and dread. The entrance exams lasted a full week. They were exhaustive and exhausting. "I am still alive," she wrote in her journal, "but so tired I don't know if it is worthwhile!" She took her English exam in the morning, in a room with sixty hopeful strangers. That same afternoon she sat through her history test—"and a hard paper it was," she remarked. The next day's schedule was even worse: agriculture, geography, French, and arithmetic, all on the same day. The following morning brought exams in Latin, algebra, and "dreaded" geometry.

Two weeks later the "pass list" appeared in the local paper. There was no possibility of slipping quietly by. Friends, neighbors, and relatives all shared the public results—exulting in triumphs, or cringing in embarrassment. Out of 264 candidates, Maud placed fifth, close to the top, and only twenty-one points shy of the highest mark.

There is no record of what her grandparents said

when they heard the good news. Maud went off by herself to the shore to celebrate alone in a "glorious evening" of a red-and-gold sunset, watching the boats pass over the water's "shimmering glory."

That same August, Maud learned that her "dear old" paternal grandfather, Senator Donald Montgomery, had died at Park Corner. He left most of his considerable property to his youngest son, James. The ever-unfortunate Hugh John received only a token sum. Maud neither expected nor received anything from the grandfather who had been so proud of her successes. Her male cousins never needed to fret about their educational expenses; their way forward was paid as a matter of course. A young woman could expect no such assistance. Help would come only from her stern, undemonstrative Grandmother Lucy Macneill, and from Maud's own efforts.

It was Grandmother Macneill alone who drove Maud off to college that September. Grandfather Alexander Macneill stayed home sulking while the elderly Lucy harnessed the horse and buggy and drove her granddaughter and all her belongings twenty-five miles over bumpy dirt roads to Charlottetown, a bustling little city of eleven thousand. They did not talk much on the drive. Once again, Maud was sorry to leave her beloved Cavendish— but she was forging her path forward.

Maud had made arrangements to board as cheaply as possible in Charlottetown. Her landlady, Mrs. MacMillan, provided tasteless food, unsanitary living conditions, and so little heat that the temperature indoors often fell below freezing. Maud piled her clothing on the bed as blankets, even using the rugs from the floor for warmth. But Maud's roommate, a lively girl named Mary Campbell, made up for the bad accommodations. Maud and Mary Campbell swiftly became close friends—and remained so. They joked about "cold ditto"—their nickname for the greasy boiled mutton they were served every day. One night Mary found a slice of soap in her bread—no extra charge.

The two young women went out boating and to the opera, on outings and picnics. They attended free lectures, including several by a well-known evangelist—a sort of early-day pop psychologist—who converted all the girls present, except Maud and Mary. Mary knew that Maud would have teased her mercilessly had she fallen in with the rest.

But before and beyond anything else, Maud dedicated herself to her studies. To save time and money, she undertook a double load of coursework—finishing two years' worth of study at Prince of Wales in one year. The wealthier girls spent three years enjoying their educations at their leisure. Maud had to earn her teaching certificate as fast as possible. Maud took fourteen classes in her one precious year at Prince of Wales, including Agriculture, Algebra, Chemistry, Geometry, Greek, Horticulture, Hygiene, Latin, Roman History, School Management, and

Trigonometry. Yet Maud loved every minute. She declared Prince of Wales College "absolutely delightful." And she still found time to write fiction and poetry.

For the first time in her life, Maud was recompensed for her work—in the form of a subscription—for a poem called "The Violet's Spell" in the *Ladies' World*. She was thrilled by this token of success. And she found another kindred spirit and supporter at Prince of Wales College—gruff Professor Caven, who not only praised her work in private but was moved to write in praise of it in public. Maud made friends among the students, too, but she was choosy. She had little patience for lackadaisical teachers, but even less for the wealthy girls who simply sat "like statues" in class.

Maud's landlady moved farther down Fitzroy Street, her new home no more accommodating than before, but Mary Campbell and Maud followed her, in a chaotic jumble of boxes. This time Maud claimed a back room on the third floor. One evening, Mrs. MacMillan ushered in an unwelcome young suitor who stayed courting for hours. It was the one time that Maud confronted Mrs. MacMillan, begging her not to let in callers unannounced—especially not this tiresome young man. If he ever came again, Mrs. MacMillan must remember that Maud was not in. "Remember!" Maud intoned sonorously, holding her surprised landlady by the shoulders—then fled the room.

Maud did entertain other, more welcome male suitors

that year, including her favorite cousin, Jack Sutherland, whom she was once caught kissing goodnight. She still received lovelorn letters from the persistent John Mustard out in Prince Albert. A young man named Lem McLeod was her most consistent escort, but Maud kept things light. She liked driving about with Lem, and thought him "a nice jolly lad." But if she saw Lem once a week, "that is quite enough for me."

In Charlottetown, Maud experienced a new kind of freedom, her energies fed by her desires and ambition. According to her own account, she slept little, ate poorly, had little or no spending money—and was never happier in her life. She tumbled from one lively event to the next, surrounded by people equally interested in books, politics, and the world of ideas.

Maud's rigorous studies provided discipline; her friends and classmates offered escape when needed. The chaos at Mrs. MacMillan's boardinghouse did not faze her. By year's end, Maud ranked sixth out of 126 students, even with her double load. She placed first in her class in English Drama, Literature, Agriculture, and School Management. This was no light accomplishment—nearly fifty students failed.

Maud's final essay was featured at that year's graduation. She wrote about Shakespeare's *Merchant of Venice,* and the Charlottetown papers made much of her speech, in both substance and delivery. Maud's speech was praised even above the speeches of the valedictorian and the lieutenant governor of the province. One article compared Maud to a teenage George Eliot, and described her essay as "a literary gem."

The Macneills were not there to hear it. Neither grandparent attended Maud's graduation from Prince of Wales. Maud passed her final exams and then, with only a few days to catch her breath, moved on to conquer the even more difficult license exams, earning a First-Class teaching certificate.

If Grandfather Alexander Macneill was impressed by any of these accomplishments, he gave no hint of it. Once again, it was only Maud's aging Grandmother Lucy who came to pick up her granddaughter and all her belongings and drive her back home alone. For once, Maud had mixed emotions coming home. She looked forward to seeing her beloved Cavendish again, yet was sorry to leave her joyful, triumphant year behind.

CHAPTER TEN

Schoolmarm in Bideford

As it turned out, not only was Grandfather Macneill unmoved by Maud's accomplishments, but he would do nothing to help his granddaughter once she returned to Cavendish. Teaching was one of the few respectable professions open to an intelligent young woman who wanted to make her way in the world—and yet the likelihood of Maud finding a job remained slim. Men were always hired before women, for higher pay, with the understanding that for women, teaching was a temporary measure before marriage, not a lifetime career. Nor were Maud's credentials strong. Maud had only one year of college, while many competing candidates had three.

Maud applied to numerous schools on Prince Edward Island, but one additional hurdle lay ahead. All of the good schools required a personal interview. Maud had to show up in person to land a job. This should have been simple enough, but Grandfather Macneill refused to drive Maud to interviews. And, not to be out-maneuvered by wife or granddaughter, he even refused them the loan of his horse and buggy.

Housebound, Maud watched helplessly as one teaching job after another went to candidates who applied in person. All that June and July of 1894, Maud fretted about where—and if—she might find employment.

Finally Maud was offered a last-minute post at the tiny town of Bideford. The pay was low, and the school small and ill-equipped. Maud was hired on a Thursday and expected to arrive that Saturday. She was filled with trepidation and hope. The night before she left home, Maud brooded in her journal about what lay ahead—"a new life among new people." She knew she would miss her "dear Cavendish"—that was a given. But, she promised herself, "if hard and persevering work can bring me good fortune," she would triumph.

Her friends Lu and Penzie drove Maud to the station at five in the morning. A storm was brewing, but the two girls kept Maud laughing and distracted. She even enjoyed the train ride to Bideford. Only when Maud laid eyes on the school itself did she draw up short. It was "about as artistic as a barn, and bleakly situated on a very bare-looking hill." That night Maud Montgomery met one of her future students—a girl almost twice as tall as herself. Maud felt like a stranger in a strange land, inadequate for the task ahead. Whenever someone addressed Maud as "Teacher," she startled and was tempted to laugh.

By Monday morning, Maud felt too frightened for laughter. She faced twenty draggle-tailed students, ages six to thirteen. Bideford was a poor community. Many of Maud's students had physical and mental challenges. The school, as she had feared from her first glimpse of it, was "big and bare and dirty"—and broiling hot in summer. The young schoolmarm Maud took down all the children's names and made a short speech, barely knowing what she said, and feeling "as idiotic and out of place as I ever did in my life."

That first afternoon Maud was ready to cry with exhaustion. But she saw that the pupils were bright and eager, if woefully unprepared. By the time she'd had tea that evening, Maud's spirits had lifted. Still in her teens, Maud possessed the irrepressible optimism of youth. She managed to find pleasant housing with the Methodist minister, his wife, and their pretty little seven-year-old daughter—one of three Mauds in her class and, as it turned out, an eager pupil. Mr. Estey, the minister, was often away from home. Mrs. Estey, his easygoing wife, was glad of Maud's company. The parsonage was beautifully landscaped and only half a mile from the school. Maud had the biggest room she'd ever known, with an open view of the bay. She quickly grew fond of Mrs. Estey and little Maud.

The Bideford community made her feel welcome at once. Maud's work as "schoolmarm" kept her too busy to be homesick during the school week. On weekends there were blueberry-picking outings, teas, dinners, moonlight drives, and picnics. And to her own surprise, Maud proved a popular teacher. Each week, more students showed up at her schoolroom door. After a month, she had gone from twenty students to thirty-eight. A few of these returning scholars were older than Maud. She was fond of them all, called them "a nice little crowd and very obliging," and they showed their affection by bringing her handpicked flowers till Maud's desk, she declared, was "a veritable flower garden."

Maud enjoyed the challenges of teaching. Not only did she encounter an ever-growing class of students of mixed abilities and ages, she also faced many other duties unconnected to teaching. The district kept her poorly supplied in kindling and in classroom necessities. Maud bought supplies out of her own pocket. It fell upon her to clean the classroom and put out the fire each night. Her teaching duties included copying out all the lessons by hand,

preparing older students for their exams, organizing recitals, grading papers late into the night, and readying herself and the students for intimidating visits from the local
school inspectors. For all of this labor she received less
than two hundred dollars for the year.

The Esteys' parsonage provided a haven after the long
work days. Unlike Maud's earlier boarding experiences
with poor food and freezing accommodations, young Mrs.
Estey ran a tidy and gracious house. She was also a good
conversationalist and an excellent cook.

One day they entertained a visiting minister, and in his
honor Mrs. Estey baked a cake. The hostess didn't realize
that she had accidentally flavored the cake with anodyne
liniment—a medicine used to soothe aching muscles.
The rest of the family stopped in horror after taking one
awful bite, while the visiting minister calmly ate his way
through the entire slice. Maud used this famous incident
later in *Anne of Green Gables,* but gave the cooking mistake
to poor Anne. Mrs. Estey more closely resembled the fictional minister's wife who gently comforts Anne over the
mistake.

Maud was less fond of *Mr.* Estey, the head of the
household, who reminded her of her hard-to-please
Grandfather Macneill. Mrs. Estey deferred to her minister husband too often and too easily, Maud thought—and
Mr. Estey didn't hesitate to impose on Maud, either. She
was expected to help fill in as organist at his Methodist

church on demand, though Maud attended services at the Presbyterian church, and all her life disliked playing music in public. Recitation was one thing—playing the organ another!

Maud made friends with a second cousin, Will Montgomery, and they had long, interesting conversations ranging from her favorite subject—books—to Russia's foreign policy, and education for the masses. One morning, Will and his family rowed Maud to Bird Island for a picnic. Someone stole the boat, and they found themselves stranded. It was a cool autumn day; all traces of warmth vanished, and the picnickers faced the prospect of staying the night on Bird Island without food or shelter. Some men poled them to a nearby island, where Will constructed his own float. They finally arrived safe back home after midnight, with Maud vowing, like her great-great-grandmother before her, to keep away from boat journeys and stick to dry land.

Whenever Maud was not busy with teaching or her new friends, she stayed in touch with her world through letters. She loved composing and receiving them—especially the "right kind" of letter, newsy and long. Mr. Mustard had finally given up his courtship, much to Maud's relief. But she heard regularly from Will and Laura Pritchard, and Mary Campbell, her old college pal from Prince of Wales.

Though Maud had a happy year teaching in Bideford,

there were times when she suffered from loneliness and gloom. Her mood swings were growing more pronounced and harder to manage. Maud had always been a girl of strong emotions—ranging on any given day from exuberance to despair. But now, approaching adulthood, her moods ran deeper, and the lows, in particular, brought her down further.

In Maud's time, there was little or no understanding of mental illness—and very poor treatment, even if she had been diagnosed. Maud's contemporary, for instance, the British writer Virginia Woolf, suffered from severe bipolar disorder, and her "treatment" was to be sent to bed early, avoid writing and company, and drink plenty of milk.

Maud turned to her journal for consolation and confession. Though still in her teens, she felt prematurely old and worn out. The "glory and the dream" seemed further out of reach, her childhood far away, especially now that she was playing the role of older and wiser teacher to others.

But Maud could still spring back from her low moods. A "rapturous reunion" with friends, a brief trip back to Prince of Wales College, a shopping expedition, an evening spent petting the parsonage cat, a moonlight drive along snowy roads gleaming like "satin ribbon"—any of these were enough to lift her spirits into near ecstasy.

That October, her male friend and escort Lem

McLeod startled Maud by declaring his passion for her. She had always thought of Lem as a lighthearted suitor, but that night he turned serious. Nor could he be dissuaded or teased away from his purpose.

"Maud, I came up here to-night to say something," he insisted. He loved her dearly, he said, and asked how she felt. Was there anyone else? Maud, compelled to be truthful, admitted there wasn't.

She was determined to get an education, she explained—at which point Lem interrupted and asked once she'd got it, wouldn't everything be "all right" between them? Maud stumbled through the rest of her refusal. She was too young to be considering marriage. "I'm young, too," Lem said stubbornly. But he was "in earnest, Maud, indeed I am. And I hope you'll consent some day." He closed by wishing her success and happiness. "I wish you well. . . . Indeed I do." His proposal was touching, dignified, and hopeless. Maud was fond of Lem, and always would be. She predicted—correctly— that he would become a successful businessman and find some other girl to marry. Still, she wrote ruefully, "It is an abominable business. . . . this telling a man you can't marry him."

A new suitor named Lou Distant came along, happy to take her out for long drives. Maud was growing cynical about her beaus. She wrote of Lou, "He is really a very handy person," but the love poems he sent her—copied word for word from popular magazines—made her howl with laughter. Lou would underline the phrases he especially liked: "She was so small, / a wee, pure bud," and so on. That didn't stop Maud from letting him escort her to parties and lectures. It didn't prevent her from accepting his gifts, either. Lou brought Maud a new novel each time he came to visit—a particular blessing, since the Methodist manse was bare of all "frivolous" reading. She and Lou had "nice jolly" chats—although, Maud noted only half kiddingly, not as satisfactory as afternoons she spent alone with poetry and doughnuts. Free time had become a rare luxury. When Maud had the chance, she would snatch a spare hour and curl up by the fire, book in hand.

That spring, the Toronto *Ladies' Journal* accepted one of Maud's poems, called "On the Gulf Shore." Her payment was in compliments and honor, she noted wryly, but she was delighted by the recognition. The *Ladies' Journal* was a popular and influential women's magazine. Every token of progress spurred Maud to greater efforts. During this busy period, she wrote hundreds of stories and poems, all the while keeping copious notes in her journal about her daily activities, thoughts, and observations.

Maud's yearnings returned to her own education as well. Her delightful year at Prince of Wales College had not opened doors as she'd hoped. She decided to try one year's course of work at the prestigious Dalhousie

University in the city of Halifax. Maud was convinced that further education would boost her writing career, and she cherished a secret hope that this move might also lead to a job in journalism. Halifax was fast becoming a center of commerce, immigration, and social change. Maud could not afford a full BA course but she believed—or tried to make herself believe—that even one year away at a "real college" in a real city could make a difference.

Maud scrimped and saved all year. Even with the cost of room and board at Bideford, she managed to save $100 out of her $180 salary. But it was not enough to cover her precious year at Dalhousie. Yet again, Grandmother Macneill came through for her ambitious granddaughter. Lucy Macneill contributed eighty dollars of her own savings to enable Maud to achieve her dream. For the cash-strapped farmwoman, eighty dollars was an enormous gift. It represented a significant portion of Lucy's life savings.

Grandfather Alexander Macneill staunchly opposed the Dalhousie plan, of course. Maud believed that even Grandmother Lucy herself did not really approve or understand. But there was nobody else to help—Hugh John still paid nothing toward his daughter's education, and Maud had limited earning power. One last time, the elderly Lucy Macneill stepped into the breach alone.

Maud finished that first teaching year in Bideford overwhelmed by affectionate going-away speeches and farewell events. She'd ended up with more than sixty students. All the schoolgirls wept to see her go, as did many grown women. Maud herself was moved to tears. The children, she wrote, had "crept into my heart." The students presented a farewell program and chipped in to buy Maud a jewelry box trimmed in silver. Each child brought a bouquet and an armful of ferns. Maud kept their good-bye speech safely tucked away in one of her scrapbooks.

Maud left Bideford in June, calling it "a very happy year," but she did not make her exit altogether unscathed. Once again, a young suitor she had thought of so little proved serious. Now it was Lou Distant, that "handy person." Maud turned him down as gently as she could, assuring Lou, as she had Lem McLeod, that he would soon forget her. This time she was mistaken. Years later she met with Lou Distant and found him a heartbroken man. Under the lapel of his tattered suit jacket he still wore a token Maud had given him years earlier.

Maud spent her summer at home in Cavendish — where for the first time in her life she felt homesick for another place. Her only friend in town now was the teacher Selena Robinson, and once Selena left for New Glasgow, Maud was bereft. Grandmother Lucy had done all she could in providing Maud with financial support; emotional support would not be forthcoming. Grandfather seethed with disapproval. Cavendish neighbors and friends clucked their amazement at Maud's plans. One woman said she couldn't imagine "what in the world" Maud needed with more education. "Do you want to be a preacher?" she demanded.

On September 16, 1895, Maud's grandmother, now in her seventies, again drove her granddaughter where she needed to go, this time all the way across Prince Edward Island to the ferry for Dalhousie, in Nova Scotia. Maud stopped and spent a relaxing night with friends in Charlottetown. But Grandmother Macneill turned the carriage around and made the long, strenuous return drive back to Cavendish without help or company.

CHAPTER ELEVEN

HALIFAX!

HALIFAX!" Twenty-one-year-old Maud printed the city's name in all capital letters in her journal entry of September 17, 1895. It was, she noted, a momentous arrival "worthy of capital letters!" Compared to Prince Edward Island, Halifax—sitting on a peninsula four and a half miles wide and two miles long—seemed to Maud a grand metropolis.

Halifax housed one of the busiest harbors in the world, feeding its shipyards, railways, and factories. The city boasted all the new modern conveniences—gas lamps, an electric streetcar system, telephones, a brand-new city hall. There were elegant neighborhoods of grand mansions, but also the immigrant poor crowded into tenements and factories. Maud saw a bustling city of extreme wealth on one hand, dire poverty on the other. The newly built Grand Theatre and Opera House accommodated two thousand spectators. Its seats were upholstered in crimson velvet, the walls hung with red and gold. Meanwhile, Chinese immigrants walked around the city carrying heavy bags of laundry on their backs, working as many as twenty hours a day.

Maud counted on Halifax to further her career. Surely, among all that hustle and bustle, someone would offer her a job in journalism or publishing. She'd left behind remote Prince Edward Island, where she suspected that even the PEI postmark on her submissions branded her as quaint and unsophisticated.

Maud's college, Dalhousie University, was a new, untested institution, almost as green as Maud herself. It was founded as a nonsectarian college in 1818, but for its first fifty years, not a single student or teacher crossed its halls. The first graduating class consisted of fewer students than Maud's one room schoolhouse in Bideford.

Maud's all-caps enthusiasm for the city wore off quickly, and just as quickly, homesickness set in. But Maud resolved to make the most of her time. While the other Dalhousie girls lived clustered together high up on what was called the "Third-and-a-Half" floor, Maud was placed below them, physically and otherwise. Many of the Dalhousie girls were well-to-do. College was merely a premarital experiment, a lark. They took their time going through their studies, while Maud again crammed two years' worth of education into one.

The Halifax Ladies' College had strict rules for its residents. The one Maud liked least—and broke most often—was lights out at ten. Many times she'd whisk herself into bed, still fully dressed, book in hand.

"It is really a hideous and depressing apartment," she mourned. The wealthy Dalhousie girls made little effort to make Maud feel welcome. The campus itself, she declared, offered only "a large ugly brick building in bare ugly grounds." She could not help comparing it to the spruce-lined woods of her little Cavendish schoolhouse, and the carefree, sociable life at Prince of Wales College.

But Maud was as eager to love as to be loved. She began tutoring the children of Chinese immigrants in her spare time. She took long walks in search of nature's consolations. Tourists flocked to Halifax's elegant new Public Gardens, with its formal gardens, fountains, and bandstand. Maud preferred the lesser-known Point Pleasant Park. There, among green trees, with a glimpse of blue water and stretches of wildflowers, she felt at home.

And Maud had a positive genius for finding beauty in unlikely places. By October Maud described her daily walk, past a hospital and poorhouse grounds, as "lovely." She worked feverishly on new poems and stories, and threw herself into sightseeing, visiting Halifax's famous monuments and attending her first-ever football game. If she could not find someone to go about the city with her, she summoned her courage and ventured out alone—and managed to enjoy herself.

Then one night in October, Maud went to bed early with an aching head. The next morning, the Dalhousie matron opened Maud's door, peeked inside, took one look and declared that Maud had come down with—measles!

One other Dalhousie pupil fell ill with measles, too, a petulant Miss Rita Perry, whom Maud had always disliked. The two unfortunates were whisked to the hospital infirmary and put to bed. They stayed in isolation for two weeks, on a strict diet of plain tea and toast. At first, Maud and Miss Perry were too sick to care, but as they began to recover, the tedium and isolation wore thin. So did the meager diet. Thrown into close quarters, the two girls came to like each other better than ever before or after—"talking freely of cabbages and kings—and men! *And* things to eat!"

The kind infirmary nurse nourished her patients by reading them stories. The other Dalhousie girls sent daily letters and stood outside their window, pantomiming the week's gossip. When Maud and Miss Perry had recovered, Maud moved upstairs to the "Third-and-a-Half" floor near the other girls, with a cozy room to herself.

Maud flung herself into her studies that winter in a valiant effort to catch up. She was determined not to waste a penny of her own money or of Grandmother Macneill's. Writing home, she emphasized the long hours dedicated to studies. But in her journal she noted with satisfaction attending a church social in a "crème-colored crepe dress with a pink silk collar" with a fillet of "pale pink silk ribbons" in her hair.

Thin and still wan from her recent illness, Maud fought homesickness every day. Staying busy helped; it was an art Maud had mastered early. By Christmas she was desperate to get home for a visit. All the Dalhousie girls were leaving.

Maud was hurt when Grandmother Macneill advised her to stay on at school for the holidays. It was wise, Grandmother wrote, to avoid the icy winter roads. Maud knew what grandmother really meant. Her visit home would be more trouble than it was worth — especially to Grandfather Macneill. "Grandfather doesn't want to be bothered meeting me or taking me back."

If she needed reminding of her status in the family, that Christmas drummed the message home. No other college girl remained unclaimed. Maud spent her holidays in the company of a few Dalhousie teachers, including a formidable Miss Kerr who, Maud maintained, "Nature must have intended as a man . . . and got the labels mixed."

Two of the teachers were feuding, and Maud was afraid to speak for fear of provoking a battle.

Yet at the end of Christmas Day, 1895, Maud declared that her holiday had been "pleasant, after all." She had eaten a good dinner and spent a social evening in the parlor. Maud was honing her special genius — to make the most of any situation, and to find humor under the most trying circumstances. It was a gift she would pass along to her own young fictional heroines, and a resource that upheld her for years to come.

One piece of Cavendish holiday news seemed small at the time. Their old, loved Cavendish minister, Mr. Archibald, had accepted a position elsewhere and was leaving after eighteen years. Maud could not have known how important a new cleric might be to her own future. At the time she merely noted, "it will seem very strange to have another minister."

Maud did well in her classes at Dalhousie, but not since studying under John Mustard had she felt so uninspired. Years later, she'd wish she had spent her precious year of freedom abroad. Still, Maud earned the highest grade on her Latin exam and placed Firsts and Seconds in all her other subjects — except English . . . which she failed! After that blow, she redoubled her efforts.

February 15, 1896, brought another wondrous first her way. Maud never forgot the date, for it marked a turning point in her writing life. For the first time ever, she was *paid* real money for her art. Maud earned five dollars — the equivalent of a week's worth of piano lessons — for a single poem. She'd won a contest run by the *Evening Mail,* answering the question "Who has more patience, man or woman?" Maud's answer, unsurprisingly, was *woman* — and she wrote her argument in verse, under the pen name Belinda Bluegrass.

Maud decided to spend those precious five dollars on something lasting, something that would remind her of her glorious achievement. She bought handsome bound volumes of poets Tennyson, Longfellow, Whittier, and Byron. A few days later she received another check from a Philadelphia magazine, *Golden Days,* for a short story. The budding writer felt delighted and encouraged — and rich!

The next two months brought a positive financial windfall. In March, Maud earned twelve dollars for a poem in *The Youth's Companion.* This was especially gratifying, she gloated, because "The Companion only uses the best things." A few days later *Golden Days* sent another three dollars for a poem called "The Apple Picking Time."

Even her Cavendish relatives and neighbors could not dismiss these successes. Literary reputation meant nothing to those honest folk. But cash was indisputable. The timing could not have been better, since Maud's experimental year at Dalhousie was drawing to an end. In April

Maud took her last exam at Dalhousie—and, she exulted, "probably the last exam I shall ever take!"

By and large, though, the year at Dalhousie proved a failure. No journalism job came Maud's way. Her ability to forge her own way in the world remained as shaky as ever. The only place to go was home. Maud left behind her cozy little room on the Third-and-a-Half floor and headed back to Cavendish—and an uncertain future.

CHAPTER TWELVE

Belmont and the Simpsony Simpsons

Once again, Maud found herself at a disadvantage because she could not interview at schools in person. Grandfather Macneill would not help Maud in this foolishness of wanting to take on the man's work of teaching. But Maud claimed a significant new supporter. It was her handsome, clever cousin Edwin Simpson, whom she had come to know a bit better during that year's visits at Park Corner.

Edwin had inherited the good looks of the Simpson family, and most of the brains. He had saved enough from his teaching to go to university. Now he made inquiries at his old school on Maud's behalf, and helped secure her his old teaching place at the Belmont community school, thirty miles from Cavendish.

Maud spent that summer with Grandmother and Grandfather Macneill. She was no longer a child—and her years of schooling were clearly over. Maud took long rambles through Lover's Lane, and visited her old church, finding it strange not to see her old minister, Mr. Archibald, at the pulpit. Upstairs in her summer den, she reread old letters, including the love letters from Nate Lockhart, and "a strong longing swept over me to go back to those dear old merry days."

A few of her childhood dreams were finally becoming reality. Maud received another five-dollar check from *Golden Dreams* for a short story. Neighbors and friends in Cavendish envied her "good luck," but few realized "how many disappointments come to one success." The young writer was beginning to recognize what a long, slow climb her Alpine path demanded.

Maud turned introspective that summer. She read philosophy and began to consider her own spiritual point of view. She dutifully went to church twice on Sundays, though she confided to her journal, "once is enough to go to church on any Sunday." Her idea of a perfect Sabbath was to escape into "the heart of some great solemn wood." There, she could commune with nature and "my own soul." But she knew better than to preach her beliefs in Cavendish. "The local spinsters would die of horror," she noted wryly.

In August, Maud set off for her teaching job in Belmont, a few miles from the home of cousin Edwin Simpson. She spent her first few nights in the Simpson household—Edwin had already left for college—observing the family. They proved a peculiar bunch. Edwin had three brothers: Fulton, a "perfect giant" with oversize hands and feet, Burton, and Alf, whom Maud found the least "Simpsony" of the bunch. There was also Edwin's teenage sister, Sophy, whom Maud dismissed as "the most lifeless mortal I ever came across." Luckily, Maud had her great-aunt Mary Lawson there for company and consolation. Aunt Mary declared that the Simpsons, having intermarried for years, were "too much of one breed."

After a few uncomfortable days with the "Simpsony Simpsons," Maud fled to board closer to her new school. The village of Belmont was picturesque, situated close to the Malpeque Bay. But her first glimpse of the people gave her a "creepy, crawly presentiment."

The Belmont school was located on "the bleakest hill that could be picked out," and student attendance was poor, with only sixteen "scrubby . . . urchins" present. The building was small and sparsely furnished; the stovepipe not yet installed. Maud arrived and found the children huddling around the cold stove, looking forlorn. Many were surprisingly backward in their studies, though one young woman, the well-to-do niece of a trustee, was preparing for Second Class work at Prince of Wales College and expected Maud to voluntarily help with all of these preparations.

Nor did Maud's lodging situation help. Her new landlady, Mrs. Fraser, was a good cook and kept a clean house, but Maud's room was barely bigger than a closet, and it was mercilessly cold. The wind whistled through the house. One morning, Maud woke to snow blanketing her pillow. The Belmont schoolhouse was little better, with a stove that worked fitfully. All Maud could think about, day and night, was how to get warm.

Maud escaped whenever possible to the Simpsons' but soon found herself part of a bizarre love triangle. She liked her cousin Alf well enough, and was happy to go out visiting and on drives. Her large, sickly cousin Fulton, however, fell into a jealous rage if Maud went anywhere with his brother. As soon as Alf and Maud stepped outside, Fulton would rush to the window to watch their every move.

Maud hated to give up the Simpsons, but she was afraid of what Fulton might do next. He spied on her, his face pressed against the window. One of her own mother's disappointed suitors, Maud remembered, had gone insane and hanged himself. Maud began to have trouble sleeping. Her only happy times were during rare visits out of town with old friends, or moments when she could sneak a little time alone with that wonderful storyteller, her great-aunt Mary Lawson.

In January Maud was permitted to move upstairs to a larger—and warmer—room at the Frasers', heated with its own pipe. Basking in warmth, Maud felt "like a new creature." That winter a visiting evangelist held revivals in Belmont every Sunday, and these, Maud granted, were welcome as entertainment against "the deadly monotony of life here." The church was so packed that they ran out of places to sit, but at least Maud's fanatical admirer, her cousin Fulton Simpson, had simmered down and now made a great show of snubbing Maud every chance he got.

Just when Maud thought she'd escaped the clutches of Simpsony love, she got a letter that startled her "more than any I ever received in my life." It was from her handsome cousin Edwin Simpson, away at college. Maud and Edwin had corresponded a few times since he'd left. His letters were always long and newsy. This one followed the usual pattern, but suddenly, in the middle of the fifth page, Edwin made a declaration. Instead of telling her in person, he had to declare in a letter "what I now feel I must tell you. It is that I love you."

Maud almost dropped the letter. She barely knew her

cousin. They'd remained near strangers since their first meeting at Park Corner. When younger, Edwin Simpson had struck her as unbearably vain and self-satisfied. He was said to be a champion debater, a fine public speaker, and his family expected great things from him. But Edwin and Maud had hardly spent two days together—far less time than she'd spent with other young men who had courted her and been turned down without a moment's hesitation.

Just when one would expect Maud to issue another swift refusal, she hesitated. That summer she had found her cousin Edwin improved from what he had once been. She judged him with an unusually cool head, given that he confessed to "an uncontrollable passion" for her. Edwin Simpson was good-looking, with his smooth dark hair and chiseled features; he was clever and well educated. Their background and tastes were similar.

Maud knew that her grandparents would disapprove. They had never cared for these Simpson relatives, and Grandfather Macneill was "rabid" against second cousins marrying. Worse still, Edwin was a Baptist—further insult to the Presbyterian Macneills. But "if I cared for him," Maud concluded, it would all "be a very suitable arrangement."

The catch, of course, was that Maud did *not* care for him. But she did not voice an absolute refusal. If Edwin pressed her for an immediate answer, Maud wrote back carefully, she would have to say no. But she might perhaps come to care for him if he were patient and willing to wait.

Edwin responded confidently. He refused her refusal. He wrote another long letter, announcing that he would wait and hope for a more positive answer. Apparently he considered himself quite a catch. Edwin had been named editor in chief of his college paper, and as a debater had been dubbed "a Hercules." His current interest was in law, he declared, and he showed every sign of one day becoming a successful lawyer. He was clever, charming, determined, and loquacious.

Stuck in poky Belmont, Maud was as lonely as she'd ever been in her life. She had fewer prospects. The new teaching work was exhausting. True, Maud was gaining a little literary recognition. One wonderful day, two of her stories were accepted by two different magazines, and that "heartened" her considerably. Yet she also wrote in the journal she only half-jokingly called her "grumble book," "Oh dear me, is life worth living?" Perhaps not, she concluded, when one felt as tired and worn out as she did.

Had Maud been less lonely, she might have paid more attention to her intuition. In those few days when she and Great-Aunt Mary Lawson had shared a room at the Simpsons', they had gone over the family one by one. Clumsy, sickly Fulton Simpson was outright peculiar, as he'd proven in his nearly demented attachment. Alf, his brother, was pleasant enough company, but he didn't dance — to Maud an "unpardonable sin." The young sister was dull.

Edwin Simpson was the best of the bunch — which wasn't saying much. He never knew when to stop bragging, or talking. He could not sit still, and his nervous tics drove Maud to distraction — he was always waving his hands, twitching, talking, and tapping his fingers. Edwin seemed to have improved in recent years, but Maud had not spent enough time with him to know if her cousin could make a possible partner.

By April Maud had come to one decision, at least: she would not return to Belmont the following year. "I hate Belmont," she declared, and the people, with very few exceptions, were "perfect barbarians." Her moods flipped from depression to hyperactivity. She was restless and nervous all that spring, and had trouble sleeping.

In the middle of April, a letter from Prince Albert brought heartbreaking news. Laura Pritchard's brother — the precious, fun-loving, lively Will Pritchard — had died suddenly, of complications from influenza. Maud felt sick with grief. She could not believe it — her merry, gentle friend from Prince Albert, the kindred spirit, gone. In agony she reread Will's last long letter to her. It felt like yesterday that they had carved their initials on an old poplar tree and walked together at twilight. Maud never admitted she had loved Will Pritchard, but thirty years after his death she had a dream that they were engaged. And when Laura Pritchard returned the little gold ring that Will had coaxed from Maud, Maud put it on her own finger and wore it till the day she died.

Maud was in a vulnerable, unsettled state of mind in the weeks that followed. When she returned to Belmont to finish the school year, Edwin Simpson showed up in person. Maud knew her grandparents would not approve. To them, this Baptist cousin would be as welcome a suitor "as if he had been a Mohammedan," but Maud had decided that when she set eyes on Edwin, if she felt she could care for him, she would accept his proposal.

She next saw Edwin Simpson to the best possible advantage—he was up on the church platform, poised and admired, addressing the Sunday school when she entered. "He looked well—spoke well." Edwin was attentive and kind, and on a moonlight walk home he urged his suit again, like a good lawyer in training. His timing was perfect. A few days earlier and Maud would have felt too unsure to answer. A few weeks later, she'd realize she "could never care for him." Caught up in the romance of the moment, Maud said yes. Edwin kissed and thanked her.

Maud came home that evening feeling dazed. She

trudged upstairs and sat a long time, dizzily staring into the dark. She was twenty-two years old. For the first time in her life, her future was secure. She felt neither happy nor unhappy, devoid of all emotion—surely not, she noted, the way a girl should feel "just parted from the man she had promised to marry."

Over the next few days, Maud realized with a creeping "icy horror" that Edwin's caresses did not merely leave her cold—they filled her with revulsion. Maud managed to put off wearing an engagement ring. Their engagement was to be a long and secret one. But her fiancé was not so easily tucked out of sight. She found evenings in Edwin's company as agonizing as those she had once spent with the determined, dull John Mustard in Prince Albert. But now her feelings of distaste were mingled with self-disgust and remorse.

Everything Maud came to learn about her fiancé made matters worse. Edwin had led Maud to believe he was headed for a successful career in law. Now that their bond was assured, Edwin revealed his true career plans—to become a minister. A Baptist minister! Maud had always declared herself unfit for a clerical life. She knew that the role of minister's wife would limit her in countless ways. Edwin offered grudgingly to give up his plans if Maud insisted, though it would be a great "inconvenience" to him. Maud quickly backed down. Edwin's future career, at the moment, seemed the least of her problems.

By mid-June Maud's stunned torpor had fizzled away. In place of numbness, she felt desperate. Maud did not love her fiancé. He irritated and disgusted her. Yet she was committed to marry the eager young man. How could she have made such an enormous mistake? She felt despairing, disoriented. "I am not Maud Montgomery at all."

Belmont buzzed with gossip about the new couple. Maud parried the teasing mechanically, but with irritation. She could not bear to be reminded of the engagement. Yes, Edwin was "good, fine-looking and clever." If their marriage consisted of nothing but intellectual conversations, she might be able to stand it. But any physical contact with Edwin felt harrowing.

Edwin's restlessness and tics and endless talking made Maud want to scream. He tired and bored her, and even worse, he seemed totally unaware of her feelings. Edwin assumed that Maud must be as thrilled by their engagement as she should be. Every fiber of her trembled "with a passion of revolt against my shackles." Even the beauty of spring failed to comfort Maud. "A veil seems to have dropped between my soul and nature." She went through the glorious June days without joy, energy, or hope. She could neither sleep nor eat. Each day was filled with increasing despair, and there was not a soul to whom she could confess her troubles.

Ending an engagement was no light matter in Maud's

world—it never is. But in her day and age, there were legal as well as social and ethical considerations. A jilted suitor had legal recourse. The scandal was highly public, and any girl who broke off an engagement would be forever branded as flighty and untrustworthy. Maud's family and neighbors had always regarded her as "queer." If she ended things with Edwin Simpson, she would only confirm their opinion. And what future prospects did she have but to shift from one poor teaching position to another, to creep from one rented room to the next?

Maud saw that spring of 1897 as a time of deep internal change. Till then, she believed she had led a relatively happy, carefree life. She had always felt buoyantly optimistic about her future. "Life looked to me fair and promising. . . . Now everything is changed and darkened."

Maud suffered her first anxiety-driven "three o'clock in the mornings" that spring. She paced up and down in her room with clenched fists, unable to sleep, unable even to sit down, picturing Edwin thinking happily of her. In a world of "beauty and gladness," she was a "blot of misery." Maud longed for home, for Cavendish—there, she thought she could find some degree of peace and calm again. In the first "dark night of the soul" in Maud's young life, her thoughts instinctively turned toward home.

CHAPTER THIRTEEN

The Year of Mad Passion

Back home in Cavendish that summer, Maud felt neither happiness nor peace, but as if she had come through a tempering fire. Autumn brought a "solemn beauty" to Cavendish, and something of its solemnity descended to Maud. She felt older than her twenty-two years — no longer young, prideful, or carefree.

She wrote, "I have begun to feel myself one with my kind." Maud always prided herself on her capability and intellect. Too often, she'd held herself aloof from the "common" folk around her. Now she knew that she could make serious blunders. Her engagement showed disastrously poor judgment. None of her breeding or wit had kept her from stumbling.

Maud was powerfully affected by the books she read that summer, and by one in particular. It was called *The Love Letters of a Worldly Woman,* and it put notions of sensuality and "earthly passions" in a new light. Maud had never thought about physical passion before—such things were too unladylike to discuss. She lived in a puritanical family. Maud's future was closing in tightly around her. She felt "gloomy at present, bounded and narrowed in." But she read with fascination about a woman who found freedom in something as taboo as sexuality.

At the same time, Maud experienced a growing curiosity about "things spiritual and eternal." She began to see that her childhood ideas of religion had failed her. Even her vision of heaven, she realized, held little promise of replenishment. One's choice seemed to be either eternal damnation or eternal boredom. Heaven, she decided, must be "dreadfully dull." The Macneills were not given to deep theological discussions; Maud had nowhere to turn in her bewilderment.

That anxious summer and fall before her twenty-third birthday, Maud realized her old beliefs had fallen away, but nothing new had yet replaced them. She grew introspective. Friendships were few and far between. She had too much time to herself, brooding and daydreaming.

Till the long engagement was over, Maud struggled to find some useful way to pass the time. Once again, Grandfather Macneill blocked all her efforts to obtain a teaching position. He proposed that Maud should clerk at a store—a more useful and "womanly" employment. When she demurred, he refused to loan her his horse to travel to teaching interviews. In early October, just when all had begun to look hopeless, Maud received a last-minute invitation to teach at a small school in Lower Bedeque—again through the intervention and help of her fiancé, Edwin Simpson.

Maud eagerly seized on this escape. Edwin Simpson's friend Alf Leard was leaving Lower Bedeque to study dentistry, and Maud stepped into his old teaching position. She also entered Alf's friendly and welcoming home as a boarder. Alf Leard had a sister, Helen, just Maud's age. The Leard homestead provided a refreshing change from the gloom of Belmont and her isolation in Cavendish. Maud entered a warm, convivial family home. Six of the Leard children still lived there—including Alf's eldest brother, Herman, a highly-thought-of young man in Lower Bedeque, preparing to take over his father's farm.

The Leard house combined the best qualities of her grandparents' house and Aunt Annie's happy home in Park Corner. The Leards were highly respected in the community, but not stuffy, nor especially intellectual. They enjoyed one another's company, going together on outings, or staying home and making their own fun. They were fond of practical jokes and appreciated Maud's ready wit and skill at storytelling. She felt at home immediately.

The only fly in the ointment was Maud's hateful engagement to Edwin Simpson, which she had not yet summoned the courage to end. Lower Bedeque provided her with a welcome respite from her anxiety.

The town sat on the south shore of Prince Edward Island, facing the mainland of Canada, giving it the feel of being connected to the wider world. There, Edwin Simpson was out of sight and out of mind. Helen and Maud quickly became friends. Maud's fourteen new students came from well-to-do farming families. She found teaching at Lower Bedeque easy and pleasant, with plenty of time left for socializing and for writing.

Several new publication opportunities came the young author's way, many in *Golden Days,* which now accepted Maud's poems and stories on a regular basis. She finally had a true literary home, as well as a comfortable, happy place to live.

Edwin continued to write faithfully to Maud. Maud dreaded Edwin's long, sentimental letters, and looked on the task of writing back as a nearly impossible burden. But at least there was distance between them. That summer, Edwin had come to Cavendish for a visit. While he'd sat chattering away in the Macneill parlor, Maud excused herself and ran up to her room. She threw herself on her bed, crying, "I can never marry him—never, NEVER, NEVER!" Then she somehow pulled herself together, walked downstairs, and went on with the visit.

Lower Bedeque was too far for Edwin to drop by for casual calls. Maud kept herself almost frantically busy. The townsfolk of Lower Bedeque had welcomed their popular, pretty young schoolteacher with open arms. So had her hosts, the Leards—and before long, one of the Leards in particular.

When Maud first met the eldest son, Herman Leard, he seemed ordinary enough—under medium height and pleasant. Maud described Herman in her journal as "slight, rather dark, with magnetic blue eyes." He did not strike her as being handsome—not at first. Herman Leard looked and acted younger than his twenty-seven years. He was easygoing and full of fun, qualities Maud always treasured in men—from her happy-go-lucky father to the still-mourned Will Pritchard. Herman drove Maud to Baptist meetings in Central Bedeque. They joked and chattered all the way there and back.

One moonlit night in November, they were making their usual drive home. Maud rode along sleepily. The stars were shining; the evening was calm and beautiful. They glided across snow. Herman said little. He suddenly drew his arm around Maud and laid her head gently down to rest on his shoulder. She made a move to protest but found herself pulled back into his embrace. Herman's warm touch triggered an electric awakening of body and mind.

That moonlight ride, she later wrote, was the beginning of her "Year of Mad Passion." Where Edwin's caresses repulsed Maud, Herman's slightest touch thrilled her. She felt happy and frightened, "voiceless, motionless." This was dangerous territory, she realized, but she had been waiting all her life for such an experience, "indescribable and overwhelming."

As soon as they reached the Leard house, Maud sprang from the buggy, running for her life. She vowed never to go near Herman again. Yet the very next evening he took her driving and put his arm around her again, drawing her warm and close. Touches turned to caresses, caresses to long kisses. Maud's passionate nature leaped to life. Poor Edwin's embraces had left her "cold as ice." Herman's first kiss "sent flame through every vein and fibre of my being." With every passing day, Maud fell more deeply under the spell of this passion. Though she did not want to admit it, she was finally, hopelessly, head over heels in love.

Maud recorded in her journal all the logical reasons why it would never work out between her and this magnetic young farmer. Even if she ended the hateful connection with Edwin Simpson, her passion for Herman Leard "seemed little short of absolute madness." He had no ambition beyond farming; he had little interest in literature or ideas. "Herman Leard was impossible, viewed as a husband." Even his attractiveness counted against him — or so Maud tried to believe; Herman was "only a very nice, attractive young animal!"

She tried to dismiss his family as being beneath her, but

the Leards were an intelligent, respected, and respectable farming family, leading citizens of Lower Bedeque, a place she liked very much. The family liked and appreciated Maud. She was crazy about Herman. What, then, was the real problem?

Maud kept a secret even from her journals, which she did not reveal in the "Year of Mad Passion"—or ever. It is the first clear instance in which her supposedly honest outpourings turn from fact to fiction. There was one important reason why Maud and Herman could not be together: he was already promised to another girl. Biographer Mary Rubio points out that Herman had been "going around" with the popular, good-looking local Ettie Schurman long before Maud came on the scene. Maud must have heard the rumors in Lower Bedeque. They were considered a perfect couple—much liked and widely admired in the close-knit community. It was understood that Ettie and Herman were soon to be married. All the while Maud was staying at the Leard house, Herman continued to squire Ettie around to church and social events.

People in Lower Bedeque gossiped that Maud made a spectacle of herself over Herman, much as poor lovesick Fulton Simpson had done over Maud—rushing from window to window whenever Herman left the house, straining to see who was with him and what time he returned. None of this earned a single word in her journals. The Herman-Ettie relationship casts a scathing light on the events of that year. Maud told herself — and therefore others — the love story she wanted to hear. Her journal reflects a whirlwind of tangled emotions: guilt and elation, excitement and dread. But the bald facts she left unrecorded.

In her journal, Maud presents herself as a young woman caught between two devoted suitors. The real facts were more complicated and less romantic. Maud and Herman both behaved badly, sneaking off behind the backs of their respective fiancés. And just when it seemed things couldn't get worse, Edwin Simpson himself dropped by for an unannounced visit.

Edwin had earlier explained that he was unable to get away for the winter holidays. He'd sent Maud her Christmas present by mail — an engraved silver knife, which he crassly informed her had cost him "quite a pretty penny." Maud was tucked away in her room in late December when Herman's sister Helen came upstairs and asked, "Who do you suppose is in the sitting room?"

Maud knew with a sinking, "horrible presentiment": it could only be the unwelcome Edwin Simpson. The Leards knew nothing of Maud's secret betrothal. Edwin presented himself that night simply as Alf Leard's school friend, so all of the Leards kept company together, little dreaming that Edwin had come to see Maud.

The sight of Herman Leard and Edwin Simpson sitting calmly side by side in the drawing room was more than Maud could stand. Had it happened in one of her books, she would have made great comedy of it. But in the thick of it, Maud lost her famous sense of humor. She bit her lips to keep from screaming.

Long after Edwin and the Leard family had gone to bed, Maud lay in the small room near Helen, feverish with despair. It was a hellish night. "There I was under the same roof with two men, one of whom I loved and could never marry, the other whom I had promised to marry but could never love! What I suffered that night between horror, shame and dread can never be told. Every dark passion in my nature seemed to have broken loose and run wild riot."

Edwin left early to catch a boat. Maud vowed to herself that she would break the detested engagement before she set eyes on him again. Meanwhile the secret lovers, Maud and Herman, resumed their illicit assignations. They found every excuse to meet. Herman would creep close to where Maud was reading by the fire and hold her hand beneath the camouflage of her shawl, or lay her book down and take her in his arms, pressing his face to hers. Maud ran her fingers through his curly brown hair. They would kiss and "all heaven seemed to open in his kisses." But later, alone in her room, she would burn with shame and confusion. Of course she confided in no one—not a relative, not a friend, certainly not Helen, who knew and liked her brother's girl, Ettie.

Maud wrote in her journal at the time, "I have . . . in

my make-up—the passionate Montgomery blood and the Puritan Macneill conscience. Neither is strong enough wholly to control the other. The Puritan conscience can't prevent the hot blood from having its way . . . but it can poison all the pleasure and it does."

Maud was never sure how much Herman understood her. She never knew how well he fathomed her heart. Surely he must have heard the rumors about her secret engagement to Edwin Simpson. Maud feared that Herman thought her nothing more than an "unprincipled flirt."

Herman himself was capable of deep feeling, Maud was sure. If he was playing with fire, she noted, he himself had been burned in this experiment. For Maud, the memory of his deep kisses, the touch of his tousled hair under her fingers, was a precious, singular gift, she wrote more than twenty years later, that she would not "barter for anything save the lives of my children." Without that year of wild passion, agonizing as it was, "all the rest of life seems grey and dowdy." She could not ever entirely deny or refute it, or wish the painful memory away. She never felt more alive than in those hours spent in her lover's arms. That was her glimpse of paradise, she felt. She never forgot it.

After Edwin's unexpected visit, Herman stayed away from Maud for a few days. He gave her chocolates and books for Christmas with a simple "These are for you, Maud." But on Christmas Eve, Herman asked if she would arrange to come downstairs with him. The next night, he came for the first time to her bedroom—ostensibly to deliver more books and chocolates. She sent him away after one impulsive, passionate kiss. But so began a pattern, almost a dance between them. The couple would keep away from each other for a few weeks, and then something would throw them together and they would end up secretly holding hands in the parlor or kissing in the privacy and darkness of her room, Herman's arms around Maud.

Herman was still seeing Ettie all this time—a fact Maud leaves out of all her written confessions. Often he came to Maud after he had been out for the evening. One fateful night, he did not come in till nearly midnight. As usual, he brought her mail and a box of chocolates, his excuse for stopping by. Maud began chattering—she was terrified of the "electrical silences" that fell between them. But that night she found herself too exhausted to go on trying to make light conversation. Herman fell silent, too.

He slipped beside her and buried his face on her shoulder. She asked him to leave. He lifted his head and their eyes locked. At that instant she felt herself on the edge of a precipice. Then he said—she doesn't record exactly what—a single sentence urging her forward. It was an invitation to disaster. Maud was young, she was Victorian, but she knew about women making love before marriage and about babies born out of wedlock. No small town in the world is so remote that it does not have its share of scandal. Maud finally lurched into action. She wept as she sent him away. "Herman — you ought to have gone long ago. Oh, go!" Even then, he stayed a moment longer, slipping onto the floor, on his knees, gazing at her. Then he kissed her and left.

Alone, she marveled at herself. Was this the proper schoolmistress, Maud Montgomery? Only a faint and hysterical *no* had stood between her and "dishonor." Maud dreaded facing Herman the next morning — but he wisely said nothing. He kept his distance a few days more, then reappeared in her room late at night, asking to borrow a light for his lamp. They went right back to their old intimate ways — embracing, touching, Maud "smoothing his curly hair with a hand that he would snatch and kiss as if every kiss were his last."

He came back again the following week. This time when she tried to send him away, he would not go. He looked at the clock, lay down beside her, and kissed her bare arm. Once again he made "the same request he had made before, veiled, half inaudible but unmistakable." For one breathless moment, her "whole life reeled in the balance."

One last time, Maud refused. It was not to save her virtue, she confessed, not from any moral sense — not even a fear of pregnancy or public shame. What held her back was "the fear of Herman Leard's contempt." If she yielded, he might despise her. She could risk anything but that.

Maud told Herman he "ought not to be here at all. Nobody ever was before. Now, Herman, go!"

This time he did not argue. He only murmured, "All right, dear. I'll go."

That night something finally broke between them. Herman may have realized that Maud was not a heartless, practiced flirt, that both were risking everything. He never came to her room again.

That spring, unexpected news from home changed everything all at once. Grandfather Alexander Macneill—Maud's stubborn, irascible nemesis—had died suddenly in Cavendish. Maud received the news with shock. She had never felt close to her grandfather—she had often feared him, but he was an essential part of her childhood, and his absence was unimaginable. She rushed home to be with Grandmother Lucy Macneill. At this crisis in her family's life, she put loyalty above longing. It was exactly the decision that her fictional Anne would make, coming home to Green Gables to care for Marilla.

Alexander Macneill's funeral was a large, solemn community event. It brought back to Maud memories of her mother's funeral in that same parlor. Grandfather Macneill, so forbidding and fearsome to Maud, appeared gentler in death than he ever had in life. Maud felt a rush of affection for the man who had been the bane of her childhood. His sister, great-aunt Mary Lawson, the wondrous storyteller, had adored him, and through her remembrances Maud could imagine the promising, clever young man he once had been.

Grandfather Macneill's death also revealed Grandmother Lucy Macneill's vulnerability. In her seventies now, the frail woman could not manage the post office alone, her only source of income. What's more, Grandfather's will left his intentions unclear—and Grandmother Lucy's position in her own house shaky.

Alexander Macneill had willed his farm to his estranged son, John, next door. Monies and household furnishings went to Grandmother Lucy Macneill. Uncle John quickly claimed the barns and horses. For the time being, it was assumed that Grandmother Macneill might stay in the house as long as she lived. But how long would the bullying Uncle John agree to this arrangement? And how could Grandmother Macneill withstand him if he began pressuring her to move out?

Maud knew that as long as she was in the picture, Lucy Macneill's position in her own house held strong. Maud made her decision at once. She would leave Bedeque as soon as the teaching year ended, and come home to help her grandmother survive. Maud could help run the post office; she would assist with the housework and upkeep and all practical affairs. And she was ready and willing to stand up to the aggressive Uncle John.

Maud's outsider status in the family was only confirmed by her grandfather's will: Grandfather Alexander Macneill had left Maud nothing at all—not even a token gift of remembrance. If Grandmother Lucy Macneill depended on Maud for her continued existence, Maud also depended on her grandmother. Neither had anywhere else to go. Together, they could preserve the homestead and their own shaky independence.

Maud acted bravely on another front as well. A few days before the news of her grandfather's death, she finally wrote to her cousin Edwin Simpson, begging release from their engagement. She made no excuses. She herself was entirely to blame, she wrote. She expected her fiancé to dismiss her with scorn.

Instead, Edwin responded with a "frantic" twenty-page letter. He wondered if she had heard rumors about him, if his letters had been too tedious. It was a heartbroken and heartbreaking piece of writing. Edwin was uncharacteristically humble and emotional. Perhaps Maud would still change her mind, he insisted. He was too in love with her to give her up easily.

Maud felt the irony of her position. With Herman, the secret lover she adored, she never knew where she stood. But Edwin Simpson truly loved her. If only she had "loved him as he loved me — or as I loved — the other man!" But Maud had suffered living in deception long enough. She had to face facts — and to get Edwin to accept them as well. Maud wrote again, begging Edwin for the pity she felt she little deserved, asking him to set her free.

Edwin responded with another long letter, this one firmer and more legalistic. He would not release Maud from the engagement, he insisted, "without sufficient reason." The fact that Maud declared she did not love him, could never care for him, and had come to feel their engagement a "hateful fetter" failed to provide enough clear evidence, apparently. Edwin proposed to set Maud free for a period of three years — but meanwhile they must continue to stay very close and to correspond. If after three years, Maud still felt she couldn't love him, then he would consent to break off the engagement.

Maud was horrified. She saw Edwin's plan as a three-year prison sentence. She wrote a bitter and angry letter she regretted instantly, but she likened herself to a wild animal caught in a trap, "biting savagely at its captor's hand." Somehow she must make Edwin understand that he was well rid of her. Her wild letter worked. A few days later, Edwin sent back her photograph. A scant handful of apple blossoms came fluttering out of the envelope — a souvenir he had claimed on a day when Maud wore a spray of apple blossom in her hair. She was free.

Herman Leard asked for a photograph to remember

Maud by. He waylaid her in their usual places, trying to find her alone. The night before she left, he held her close and they passionately kissed good-bye. She could hardly bear to tear herself away. Her love for Herman proved to be messy, bewildering, exhausting, foolish—and eternal. She never forgot him. Heartsick, Maud felt her life was over—and more than half wished it was. Her season of great passion would never come again.

Herman Leard stood among the others at the station the next morning to see her off. There was no time or place for a personal farewell. His slender figure was the last she saw receding at the platform.

CHAPTER FOURTEEN

Back in the House of Dreams

Maud could not have known when she rode away from Lower Bedeque that she would be trapped at home for most of the next thirteen years. If she had known, she might not have had the courage to begin. Maud spent a wretched first week in Cavendish, heartsick for Herman, missing Bedeque, which now seemed, in hindsight, a beautiful oasis in her lonely existence.

Maud had returned to her childhood place only to feel trapped by old childhood roles. Her aging grandmother assumed Maud would live exactly as she herself did. Lucy Macneill had grown increasingly nervous and set in her ways. If she went to bed at nine o'clock, she expected her young granddaughter to go to bed at nine. If she bathed once a week, then Maud must only bathe once a week.

Maud felt isolated, "a virtual stranger" in Cavendish—so many friends in her beloved old crowd were gone. She escaped, as always, into books and nature. She reread her old letters, burning many. She looked over her lighthearted journals from the past, marveling at how merry and easy her life had been.

But her true apprenticeship as a writer also began during these difficult years. Without teaching, without the fetters of an unwanted engagement, without social distractions, Maud bent her full energies to writing. She knew how to work long hours. She was not afraid to fail—she was used to that now, too. She earned new literary successes to lift her spirits—letters of acceptance and invitations to send further work—and the writing itself was "a great comfort to me in these sad days." Maud was back in her beloved upstairs summer suite of rooms, overlooking poplar and fir woods, fields of red clover. It may have been the only place in the world that could have healed her broken heart. "The house is still, the atmosphere one of dreams," she wrote.

Over the next two years, one harsh reality hit after another, a series of blows. In summer of 1899, a year after she had left Bedeque, she heard the shocking news that her magnetic, mysterious, vibrant young lover, Herman Leard, had died suddenly of influenza. Grandmother Macneill read about it in the local paper. Knowing nothing of Maud's passionate history with Herman, the older woman mentioned it casually.

Maud's initial reaction in her journal was intense, wild, filled with raging sorrow. It was easier, she confessed, to think of him as dead, "mine, all mine in death, as he could never be in life, mine when no other woman could ever lie on his heart or kiss his lips."

All of Maud's hidden jealousy burst out upon the news of Herman's death. And of course it was Ettie Schurman whom everyone remembered at the funeral and afterwards. Ettie grieved for Herman long and truly. She planted blue forget-me-nots on his grave. All of Bedeque mourned Herman and pitied poor Ettie. Herman's funeral was a large one. But Maud had no part in any of it. The newspaper announcement of his death went into Maud's scrapbook. Maud had no photo to remember him by, so she cut a picture from a popular magazine of a dreamy-looking dark-haired young man in uniform she claimed was "as like him as if it had been his photograph." As archival photographs of the real Herman reveal, the clipping barely resembled the young farmer at all.

Now that Herman was in the spirit world, would he know how much Maud had adored him — how deeply he'd entered her heart? The thought terrified her, but nearly as unbearable was the thought that his ghost would sweep coldly by her, "as some chill, impersonal spirit." Maud wished herself "lying in Herman's arms, as cold in death as he."

For the rest of that year, Maud struggled without success to regain her composure. She tried to resume an old way of life that no longer fit a maturing young woman. Maud visited with relatives, joined the local sewing circle, attended pie socials, and involved herself with the Cavendish Literary Society — but what had been so dear to her as a child had lost its savor. She felt old and lonely, an outsider at the edge of spinsterhood. While her neighbors socialized, Maud fled to the woods. Other young people were wild for the new hobby of bicycling, but Maud took up photography. She wrote poems and stories, and read "like a book drunkard," for she now selected the books for the Cavendish Lending Library.

January of 1900 brought news of yet another, even more shocking death. This, too, would tip the balance of Maud's existence. The telegram from Saskatchewan read simply: "Hugh J. Montgomery died today. Pneumonia. Peacefully happy and painless death."

Maud was stunned into silence by her father's death. For most of her life, she had struggled without either parent nearby. Now Maud was fully an orphan. She could not write one word about her father's death for six months. Even her ambition as an author seemed to die with Hugh John. Though he lived so far away, Maud had always taken comfort in the knowledge that her father was in the world somewhere, loving her, proud of her.

She wrote, in lines no biographer has ever read without a terrible sense of pity and irony, "Have you left your 'little Maudie' all alone? That was not like you." In truth, it was exactly what her father had been doing all her life.

Maud was only twenty-five, but she had suffered deep losses: her young mother, her dear friend Will Pritchard, Grandfather Macneill, the longed-for yet inaccessible Herman Leard, and now her "darling father" as well. This final severing sank her into a lifeless grief for months — but it may have freed her as well. Maud knew beyond the shadow of a doubt that she must "henceforth face the world alone."

Words were her salvation, her business, and her hope. Little by little, her art returned to her. Maud took stock of herself with a cool eye. She tallied up her debits and her strengths. She had few financial resources — her late father had left her two hundred dollars, and she had another hundred in savings; she possessed a "scanty and superficial education" and just enough training to be a poorly paid teacher. "I have no influence of any kind in any quarter," she declared frankly.

But Maud was young and energetic. She loved life, for all its sorrows. She believed in herself, if no one else did. She had, she was sure, a "knack of scribbling." Each year she had made a little more money by her pen. That year she had earned nearly one hundred dollars. It was not enough to get by—but financial independence was drawing closer. Maud had fierce energy. She had a gift, people said, for making things happen. She would face the future, she determined, with "an unquailing heart."

That summer an unlooked-for opportunity came her way. As an ambitious college student at Dalhousie, Maud had yearned for an entry into a newspaper career. Now, these many years later, an old acquaintance from Dalhousie wrote to Maud to say that the *Halifax Echo,* the city's evening newspaper, was looking for a proofreader. Might Maud be interested?

Maud would be paid five dollars a week—more than she had ever earned as a teacher. The temporary job could lead to better prospects. She and Grandmother Macneill agreed it was too good an opportunity to pass up. Maud arranged for her cousin Prescott to stay in the house with Grandmother while she was away.

The prospect of leaving Cavendish rekindled Maud's energy and made her "industrious and respectable" all summer. She "piped and danced to other people's piping," involving herself in every church activity, as well as dedicating herself to the gardening, cooking, baking, and domestic handicrafts her grandmother valued.

Maud had found a regular audience in the publishers of juvenile fiction, in church-related magazines, and now she wrote her stories to order—not the kind she liked best, she admitted, "a rattling good, jolly one," but those with morals tucked neatly inside. She added new magazines to her list of publications, and applied herself to please each editor in turn. Her output was prodigious, the hours long and late, but "Oh, I love my work!" she exulted.

Maud came to Halifax for her interview in September, expecting to stay only a few days. Instead, she landed the newspaper position at once. Maud's next-door cousin Prescott reluctantly agreed to keep his grandmother company for the winter.

In busy Halifax—no all-caps this time—Maud struggled first with homesickness and then, as she had increasingly each year, with the depressions that plagued her every winter. Maud likely suffered from a condition now known as seasonal affective disorder. In her time, there was no name for the condition, no acknowledgment of its reality, and no treatment. Like clockwork, Maud's mood would begin to darken in November, right around the time of her birthday, worsen with the onset of short winter days, and improve only when the sun and warmth returned in late May or June. She felt lethargic and exhausted in the winter, overwrought and restless in spring and summer. Her cyclical symptoms may have been one manifestation of her ongoing manic depression, guided strongly by the absence or presence of sunlight.

But Maud had no time to sink into depression. She must make good in her new role as a newspaperwoman. Maud was the only woman on the *Echo*'s editorial staff. In addition to proofreading, Maud became a kind of verbal handywoman for the paper. She copyedited, answered the telephone, composed her own column, and covered all the society events—no obituaries allowed. "Evidently funerals have no place in society," she noted tartly.

Maud worked at an early form of publicity and promotion—clipping editorials from the morning paper and sending them out. She began interviewing local businesses, writing up puff pieces praising local stores. One pleased milliner sent Maud a complimentary new hat, which she accepted with delight. That "miracle," as she described it, never repeated itself again.

Maud's column in the *Echo* was called "Around the Tea Table," and published under the pen name Cynthia. It was a light catchall for everything from local tourist attractions to fashion trends and hobbies. When no society letters were forthcoming, it was Maud's job to invent them—her least favorite job.

Now and again the *Echo* ran a serial novel in the paper. One time it was "A Royal Betrothal," a romance about the

British royal family. When the end of the story got lost in the mail, Maud was ordered to create an ending. She protested that she knew very little about romance writing— or the royal family. The editor insisted. Maud was amused to hear two women on a train talking about how the story that had seemed to drag on forever quite suddenly came to a lively conclusion. From then on, whenever the newspaper ran into trouble with one of its serials, Maud stepped in to save the day.

Maud still found time to write her own juvenile potboilers. She was not proud of the literary quality of this work, but it brought in more money than she was making on the newspaper. And now and again she still wrote what she considered "a fit and proper incarnation of the art I worship."

Maud moved around in bustling Halifax without feeling at home. She combated constant depression and homesickness. "There is no loneliness like the loneliness of a crowd," she noted. Her bedroom view was always of dreary backyards. But, as usual, Maud fought back against the gloom. She rediscovered an old girlfriend from her college days. She became "chums" with a girl in the business office of the *Echo*. And when she had no choice, she set off alone on streetcars and long walks around Halifax. Maud attended her first Universalist Church service, which felt more like "a lecture and concert" than a religious event. Even her misadventures had a way of looking like fun in hindsight—and all was material for her art.

Maud blossomed in this newfound freedom. She could think and write what she pleased, with no one to censor or contradict her. She poured her thoughts and observations into her journal. It's there, in the pages of her journal, rather than in her juvenile potboilers, that one sees the author's humor, sharp eye, and true descriptive genius emerging. The future king and queen of England, she noted, were unimpressive—the duke "an insignificant man with a red nose." The duchess, she declared, "looks to be the best man of the two."

By May, Maud's winter doldrums had passed. Her thoughts returned, as always, homeward to Prince Edward Island. Though Maud enjoyed her newspaper work, she had grown no fonder of crowded Halifax. And she heard that cousin Prescott and Grandmother Macneill were not getting along. Maud suspected her cousin of treating her grandmother shabbily. Once again, duty pulled her home. This time, Maud vowed not to leave as long as she could be of use to her grandmother. A woman of her word, Maud would prove faithful to the very end.

On her return, Maud discovered that Uncle John had been pressuring Grandmother Macneill to give up the house. He hoped she could be farmed out to one of her other children, and that his son, Prescott, would take over the old homestead. When Grandmother Macneill and Maud resisted, Uncle John reacted with characteristic brutality. He cut them off completely.

Though he lived next door, he would not lift a finger to help them. He seemed to take pleasure in creating obstacles to their happiness and comfort. His anger was relentless. He never again visited his mother till she lay on her deathbed—but he did a great deal to worry and trouble her till then.

Maud provided whatever social life came into the old homestead. She kept herself and Grandmother Lucy active in the church. Maud cooked and cleaned, did the heavier chores that were considered "man's work," and helped run their post office. No one in the family offered to help, not even for a day. If the Macneills had hoped to weaken Maud's resolve, they'd chosen the wrong woman. Maud only became more determined, and even the frail, elderly Lucy Macneill dug in her heels.

Maud's loyalty was immediately rewarded on an important front. There were few of her old "kindred spirits" left in Cavendish. Maud's childhood friend Penzie had grown up and away in tastes and interests, becoming a regular matron. Nearly all of Maud's close female friends had married, and most male friends had left the island. But a new teacher named Nora Lefurgey arrived in town that fall. Nora was lively, intelligent, attractive, independent, and full of fun. Maud called her new friend "a positive God-send." They were matched in everything, and that in itself in tiny Cavendish, Maud declared, had "a flavor of the miraculous."

In winter, Nora came to board at the Macneills'. Maud and Nora were both unmarried, handsome women in their mid-twenties—an age where others had begun looking upon them as hopeless spinsters. But they did not see themselves that way. They kept a joint journal together, filled with lighthearted teasing, sharp commentary, private jokes, and nonsense. They wrote about the few potential suitors in town, accusing each other of being in love with one or another of all the eligible men. It's in this shared journal, in 1903, that we first read about Ewan Macdonald, the visiting minister to the Cavendish church. Maud noted that she'd gone alone to the Thursday night church meeting, since Nora had a cold. She wanted to take her own close look "at our new 'supply.' Who knows but that he is the 'coming man,'" she wrote jokingly.

"This morning we had a Highlander to preach for us and he was 'chust lovely' and all the girls got stuck on him. My heart pitty-patted so that I could hardly play the hymns. It's weak yet so I shall stop short."

She also wrote her first impressions of the "chust lovely" new minister, but later scissored those pages from her journal and destroyed them. It's safe to say that Ewan

Macdonald struck Maud as no more than one of a dozen men lightly regarded, worth teasing about, and then moving quickly past.

The same year she met Nora, 1902, Maud was introduced by a mutual friend to two long-distance pen pals she would count as close friends all the rest of her life. Both men were bachelors when Maud "met" them by mail; each became an essential connection, someone to whom she could safely pour out her feelings on life, love, and literature.

One was Ephraim Weber, a Mennonite teacher and homesteader in Western Canada. Weber aspired to be a writer. He was "an ideal correspondent," Maud found, to her surprise, and his letters were "capital" on a wide range of intellectual subjects. Her second pen pal was the gentle George MacMillan, a Scottish journalist. MacMillan's letters were not as brilliant as Ephraim Weber's, but Maud suspected "as a man, he is superior to the former." Each new long-distance friend was lonely, articulate, and book-loving, which made them ideal correspondents.

When Maud was not ensconced in nonsense with Nora—or taking photographic "snaps," writing, or going for swims in the Saint Lawrence—she easily lapsed into loneliness and gloom. Domestic and financial anxiety haunted Maud and Grandmother Macneill in these years. They lived right next door to Uncle John, yet were severed from him as effectively as if they had been banished to another country. Uncle John owned the barns on their old homestead but refused to let Maud and his mother keep a horse and carriage. The two women were forced to depend on others for even the most basic transportation.

Sometimes, in an especially dark mood, Maud would read over the jokes in those shared daybooks with Nora and wonder how she could be one of its authors. "I'm tired of existence," Maud confided to her journal.

She never completely recovered from her "year of mad passion" with Herman Leard. Regret haunted her. "Life has been a sorry business for me these past five years." But no one guessed the depth of her sadness. Maud was good at putting a bright face to the world. She knew she was considered a "very jolly girl," but she often gave way to despair. Maud was in her late twenties now, and in her darkest moods she felt little hope for the future: "Life will just go on getting a little harder for me every year. . . . Soon youth will be gone and I shall have to face a drab, solitary, struggling middle age. It is not a pleasant prospect."

By summer of 1903, Nora Lefurgey had finished her teaching stint and fled Cavendish. Maud cast about for new friendships. That September, the thirty-four-year-old Ewan Macdonald, the "chust lovely" new up-and-coming minister, took on the ministry at the Cavendish church. He stopped by the Macneill post office for chats with Maud, and those lighthearted conversations soothed them both.

Maud earned $500 from her writing that year. She

experienced the delicious novelty of magazine editors *requesting* new work. Maud's name cropped up in an article about the rising authors of Canada. Though she little suspected it, Maud was laying the foundation for her most famous house of dreams.

The brutal winters between 1902 and 1905 brought the worst snowstorms in Prince Edward Island history. All mail stopped. No visitors came by for days. Snowdrifts piled as high as the top of the old house on either side. The ground-floor rooms were as dark as dusk. The wind howled around the old homestead, keeping Maud a prisoner indoors. As soon as she could get outside and walk again, in the flaming red and gold of a winter sunset, Maud could "forgive" the storm—only to be trapped by the next blizzard.

The long-awaited, much-delayed spring released "a sheaf of happy days." Maud was almost incapable of being unhappy in June. All winter she planned out her garden; as soon as weather permitted, she worked with her hands in the dirt. A walk through Lover's Lane could make her breathlessly happy. She felt the reassuring presence of the sky and sea: "I gazed always on the splendid pageant of the sea—splendid with ever-changing beauty of dawn and noon and midnight, of storm and calm, wind and rain, starlight, moonlight, sunset."

The escape into certain stories reliably uplifted her. One such volume was Washington Irving's exotic

Alhambra, which Maud had devoured as a girl. At the end of one dreary day she wrote, "Washington Irving, take my thanks. Dead and in your grave, your charm is still potent enough to weave a tissue of sunshine over the darkness of the day. I thank you for your 'Alhambra.'"

All too often, books were the only company Maud *could* entertain. Grandmother Macneill was fiercely jealous of Maud's friendships. As she aged, the old lady became increasingly fretful and withdrawn. Lucy Macneill never made anyone feel welcome in their home, and she restricted access to it as much as possible. Though Maud was earning enough to make repairs to the old homestead, Grandmother Macneill would allow nothing to be changed. She would not even permit Maud to bake a cake when company came. The two women spent more and more time alone.

But Maud loved the old homestead and was fiercely protective of it. She took comfort in all her "little hobbies"—gardening and photography, scrapbooks and handicrafts. She managed to involve herself in the life of Cavendish in a dozen ways, large and small: became the church organist and choir director, taught Sunday school, engaged in the Literary Society and Lending Library. In those years of isolation from the larger world, Maud came to know her neighbors in a deeper, more intimate way, as her fiction shows time and again.

Life, she later argued, was just as vivid in small towns as in big cities. Maud knew her best subject matter lay not in faraway places but right at home. In these long, lonely Cavendish years, she was digging deep among the roots of her own home soil—all she needed was the dropping of a seed.

CHAPTER FIFTEEN

The Creation of Anne

In 1904, Maud came across an old note scribbled in her journal: "Elderly couple apply to orphan asylum for a boy. By mistake a girl is sent them."

Over the next eighteen months, Maud began to shape around this brief entry her most famous novel, *Anne of Green Gables*. Anne Shirley, the red-haired orphan who shows up at the railway station of Avonlea, captivated Maud's imagination. She fell in love with her own heroine—and no wonder. Maud performed the great alchemy of art. She transformed her own history of abandonment into a story of rescue. Maud put herself into the fictional Anne: her own vivid imagination; a passionate love of nature; her habit of naming inanimate objects; the imaginary cupboard friend; her hungry affection for books; her own vanity, pride, stubbornness; and a deep, abiding attachment to those she loves.

The novel's setting, Avonlea, is Maud's hymn to small-town life in Cavendish. Avonlea is a pastiche of every place Maud knew best, from Lover's Lane, that flowery path that she loved "idolatrously," to the Haunted Wood. The Lake of Shining Waters was based on the bright pond Maud glimpsed from her guest bedroom at Park Corner. The White Way of Delight, Violet Vale, and the Dryad's Bubble were pure inventions.

The germ of Anne's story, jotted in Maud's old journal, echoes the history of Maud's adopted cousin, Ellen Macneill. Ellen had arrived by train with her brother, instead of the expected two boys from the orphan asylum. Another man adopted the brother at once. Maud's elderly cousins, Pierce and Rachael Macneill, decided to adopt the three-year-old girl. Seventeen-year-old Maud wrote about it in her journal—then let the idea rest quietly for years. She denied any parallel between her own invented Anne and Ellen Macneill, whom she unkindly dubbed "one of the most hopelessly commonplace and uninteresting girls imaginable."

Anne's house, Green Gables, was loosely based on a house belonging to two other cousins, David and Margaret

Macneill. Their house was notoriously untidy, nothing like Marilla's well-swept home. The real-life David Macneill was shy and retiring, and this older couple, too, had adopted—David and Margaret had taken on the raising of an illegitimate great-niece. Maud noted that the book illustrations of Matthew Cuthbert looked uncannily like David Macneill, though she hadn't consciously thought of him while creating Matthew.

One may find hints of Maud's father's shy and affectionate nature idealized in Matthew, just as Grandmother Lucy Macneill's flinty personality is elevated into the lovable Marilla. But Maud argued rightly that no writer simply plucks her characters from life. Fiction is the art of transformation. For many writers, including L. M. Montgomery, it allows for happy reconciliations they cannot achieve in real life.

Marilla Cuthbert possesses the keen sense of humor and understanding that Grandmother Lucy Macneill lacked. Unlike Maud's real-life father, Matthew Cuthbert is a model of devoted fatherhood, immensely brave when it comes to protecting his girl. And the fictional Anne loves the right young man in the end, overcoming her own stubbornness and false pride. Anne Shirley earns the happy marriage that Maud found so hard to achieve. *Anne of Green Gables* sparkles with happiness all around, though it's touched by heartbreaking sadness. And that is true especially of its mercurial heroine, Anne, who makes us laugh one instant and cry the next.

Margaret Atwood, a well-known Canadian author, has argued that the main love story in *Anne of Green Gables* plays out not between Anne and Gilbert Blythe, but between Anne and the love-starved elderly Marilla. Certainly Marilla's tart personality gives savor to Anne's sweetness. Without Marilla, Anne might strike the reader as almost too good, despite her misadventures.

Anne of Green Gables is a book about creating lasting family. It is a celebration of place, a story about belonging. No one but Maud Montgomery, with all her checkered history and heart-hungry longing, could have created it.

Maud found her inspiration when she was most ready to use it. By 1905, the shy new minister, Ewan Macdonald, had moved full-time from nearby Stanley to Cavendish — closer to the Cavendish Church, and to Maud. He had recently escaped a near engagement to another woman and so proceeded very slowly with Maud. Their friendship was founded on common interests. Maud acted as church organist and director of the church choir. She and the young minister — just four years her senior — always found plenty to talk about. Nora wrote teasingly about Maud's sudden interest in church events and ice cream socials, "You know she has taken up church work since the young ministers have struck the place."

Aside from the few joking entries in Maud and Nora Lefurgey's notebook, we don't have Maud's true first impression of Ewan Macdonald. Ewan admitted that he had his "eye on her from the beginning." He was wise to proceed cautiously. Maud was skittish in the face of courtship, but she hungered for friendship. Ewan was sweet-tempered, with dimples, an attractive smile, and that irresistible Gaelic lilt in his voice. He was considered the catch of Cavendish — every unmarried girl or woman for miles around had set her sights on him.

Ewan was Prince Edward Island–born and –bred. But he came from a large farming family on the other side of the island. His family was less prosperous than Herman Leard's, and Ewan's upbringing had been far less elegant than Maud's.

Like Maud, Ewan had attended both Prince of Wales College and Dalhousie University. Two of his brothers became farmers, but Ewan was the treasured intellect of the family, and his desire to become a minister was seen in his family as a significant step forward. In 1903 he began regularly guest preaching in Cavendish, and by 1905 he was inducted as full-time minister. Other aspects of Ewan's biography remain less clear. He seems to have had a youthful history of clinical depression, a fact he managed to keep well hidden from Maud.

Between 1903 and 1905, Ewan boarded in nearby

Stanley. Maud frequently visited Stanley, for another love of her life now lived there—her youngest Park Corner cousin, Frede Campbell.

Cousin Frede was ten years younger than Maud. That age difference had kept them apart in childhood and youth. For years they maintained a casual, friendly family relationship, as one might expect of one cousin a decade older than another. Then during one memorable visit at Park Corner, Maud and Frede stayed up talking and discovered themselves like-minded on a wide range of subjects—true and absolute kindred spirits. It was a hot summer's night, and the two cousins talked till the cool of dawn. From that night forward, they lovingly stood by each other. Maud adored Frede. She called her "my more than sister." Between Ewan and Frede, Maude had found two essential people, and they buoyed her up while *Anne of Green Gables* was taking shape.

For someone who kept such careful journal notes on her private thoughts and life events, Maud revealed very little about her writing process. She may have begun notes on her masterwork as early as 1904 and probably finished it in the winter of 1906. She likely took between nine and eighteen months to finish the novel.

In 1905, she told her Mennonite pen pal Ephraim Weber that she wrote three hours a day—one hour of magazine work in the morning, one hour of typing in the afternoon, and one hour for novel composition in the evening. The rest of her time was eaten up by housework. She wrote fast, she told Weber, "having 'thought out' plot and dialogue while I go about my household work." Yet the young writer published forty-four short stories in 1905—a lifetime's worth of work for many authors—and she wrote most of *Anne of Green Gables* that same year.

When Maud rediscovered her note about the elderly couple, she quickly sketched out a seven-chapter story—the ideal length for a Sunday-school magazine submission. She gave her main character a name, Anne Shirley. She clipped a picture of a redheaded girl from a magazine and modeled her character on that image. Then she set to work.

Ewan Macdonald interrupted the opening chapter that June afternoon when he stopped by for his mail. Maud and Ewan chatted till the light of day had faded from the kitchen. Maud must have felt sure both of her subject and of her visitor's interest.

Most of the composition of *Anne of Green Gables* happened not down in the busy Macneill kitchen/post office but in Maud's flight of rooms upstairs. The central character of Anne Shirley swiftly took on a life of its own. Even the all-important *e* at the end of her name flashed into Maud's mind at once. Anne "took possession of me to an unusual extent." And then the daring thought came to Maud. "Write a book. You have the central idea. All you need do is spread it out over enough chapters."

Anne of Green Gables was not Maud's first attempt at a novel. She had written an earlier book called *A Golden Carol,* a preachy and predictable story about an idealized girl named Carol Golden. It was just the kind of fiction Maud disliked, and she ended up burning it.

Anne of Green Gables is about a perfectly *imperfect* girl—stubborn, homely, impulsive, proud—who is always getting into scrapes. Anne has a bad temper; she can hold a grudge. She is hypersensitive about her red hair, equally vain about her nice nose; she is by turns ecstatic and despondent, brilliant and silly, brave and tremulous. Anne Shirley felt vibrantly real to Maud. Maud knew the whole book relied upon her young heroine. As she would later write, "Books are not written about proper children. They would be so dull nobody would read them."

Maud confided to her pen pal George MacMillan that, of all her works, this was most truly her own voice and style. The prose of *Anne,* she maintained, is "my real style," and the fact that it was her own natural voice was, she believed, "the secret of her success." Other stories may have been skillfully constructed, but they felt "created rather than summoned," to quote another children's writer, P. L. Travers. During spring and summer of 1905, Maud poured out the first six chapters of the novel—the section leading up to the moment when Marilla and Matthew decide to adopt Anne.

We don't know the details of daily composition, but

Maud's journals give us a glimpse into her state of mind. That June, the world bloomed for her. Maud responded to human warmth as strongly as she did to sunshine. She had two close friends nearby, Frede and Ewan. She wrote quickly and easily in her white room overlooking fields and gardens.

Only two years earlier, Maud had confided to pen pal George MacMillan her secret fear: "I can never be a really great writer." She genuinely believed her novel might appeal to only a handful of young female readers; she warned pen pal Ephraim Weber not to expect anything great or mighty when he read the book. But she also noted to MacMillan, "I think we should just write out what is in us—what our particular 'demon' gives us—and the rest is on the knees of the gods. If we write truly out of our own heart and experience that truth will find out and reach its own."

That June, while working on *Anne of Green Gables,* Maud sat at the window of her den, looking out on "a wide green field lush with nearly sprung clover, a lane where I know purple violets are growing thickly and an orchard arrayed as if for a bridal." She added, "It is just good to be alive in a world where there are Junes."

The creation of Anne marked the June of Maud's life: the flowering of her gift as a writer, and the fulfillment of hope. She was supported by the nearness and warm affection of Frede and Ewan, though neither knew that she was at work on her first book. As some astute readers have observed, *Anne of Green Gables* takes us through five full years of Anne's young life, but more than half of the novel's events take place in the month of June. The novel was even published in June.

Maud was not the only one flourishing during this period. Ewan Macdonald, uplifted by his friendship with Maud, was fast becoming a popular minister. Together they began a few local beautification projects, including at the graveyard where Maud's mother was buried. The young minister received invitations to give sermons in nearby Charlottetown and farther afield. Other clerics had started their ministries in Prince Edward Island and left for larger, more prestigious churches. Ewan thought his own career might benefit from some additional education. He made plans to study abroad.

On the evening of October 12, 1906, Ewan drove Maud into the country to visit friends. Along the way, he confided his plans to leave Cavendish in order to study at Trinity College, in Scotland.

Maud had begun to think of the shy minister more seriously. She celebrated his successes; she was proud of their friendship, and of his obvious fondness for her. It had occurred to her that Ewan might at some point propose marriage — but she remained noncommitted. She was not wildly in love with him the way she had been with Herman Leard. Ewan stirred no fires in her. But she had come to dread unbridled passion. When it came to men, Maud had few instincts to go by, little real-life experience—and as usual, no one to consult. It's probable that Grandmother Macneill and Frede knew and liked Ewan. And it's almost certain that Maud had confided some of her feelings to Frede. But she had never had a single close male relative she could entirely confide in and trust. That half of the human race remained a mystery.

Ewan's talk about his plans on the carriage ride made his upcoming departure seem suddenly real. He was going away, to another country—another continent. Maud had enjoyed the ease of his company. She was intrigued by his dimpled smile, and she felt his attraction as a man. But she also knew she could never marry as long as Grandmother Macneill was alive—to abandon the elderly woman now was unthinkable.

There was another fly in the ointment: Maud felt no desire to become a minister's wife, any more than she had wished it with the unfortunate John Mustard or the detested Edwin Simpson. A cleric's wife was hemmed in on all sides. Why, she would not even be allowed to play whist! she noted with dismay. Maud loved to dance and have fun; to go out driving, dress up in fashionable clothing, attend parties, and have adventures. All this and more would be frowned on in a minister's wife.

In Maud's "three o'clock in the morning moods" of despair, she thought she had better marry no matter whom, no matter when. But by day, she thought it "wiser to keep my freedom and trust life." All in all, she concluded, she did not "care enough for Ewan Macdonald to justify my marrying him."

As Maud and Ewan drove in silence together that October night through the dark and rain, Ewan suddenly spoke up: "There is one thing that would make me perfectly happy, but perhaps it is too much to hope for. It is that you should share my life—be my wife." Maud came to her own surprising realization. She could not lose him. Ewan had become an essential part of her existence. Somehow, she felt, "I could not let him go out of my life. He seemed to belong in it."

Maud agreed that if Ewan would wait, she would marry him. The engagement would be secret—and it might be long. She couldn't abandon her aging grandmother. Indeed, the engagement stretched out for five years. Maud wore the little diamond solitaire on her left hand only at night, in the privacy of her upstairs room. She felt, in her own word, "content." The engagement might not stir joy—certainly not the ecstasy she had felt in Herman Leard's arms — but it seemed the beginning of a new, secure happiness.

And meanwhile, what had become of *Anne of Green Gables*? After Maud completed the novel, she faced the daunting prospect of having to type up the whole thing in order to send it out. Maud used an ancient typewriter that didn't print legible capital letters and could not print the letter *w* at all. She had to go back and fill in every single *w* by hand.

First the hopeful young author sent her book off to a new American publishing company. The rejected manuscript bounced right back. Next Maud mailed *Anne of Green Gables* to an older, more established Canadian firm. The older company sent it back, too. Maud was grateful that her family ran the post office. At least no one in town need know about these embarrassing rejections. She tried three other "betwixt-and-between" publishing houses, and all three sent it back. Of the five rejections, four were form letters. The fifth contained a terse note: "Our readers report that they find some merit in your story, but not enough to warrant its acceptance."

Discouraged, Maud hid the *Anne* manuscript away — for good, she thought, dumping it in an old hatbox. At some later date, she decided, she might take it out, polish it up, and boil it back down to the original seven chapters deemed fit for a Sunday-school magazine. Down the line, she might earn thirty or forty dollars for it.

Maud was cleaning out her room the following year when she came across the *Anne* manuscript. She reread the novel and liked it enough to tell herself, "I'll try once more." This time she sent it to the L. C. Page publishing company in Boston, Massachusetts. While she waited for an answer, Maud put the book out of her mind.

Maud had more pressing and worrisome thoughts that winter. Ewan Macdonald was struggling alone in far-off Glasgow. His inner turmoil began almost as soon as he arrived in Scotland. Whatever energy Maud had inspired in her fiancé deserted him once he was out of her sight. He found his fellow students unfriendly and felt himself inferior and unworthy.

Ewan quickly fell into the religious melancholy that would periodically plague him all the rest of his life. His academic failures, he felt, were proof of condemnation from God. He started skipping classes. Maud urged him to seek help, but he was convinced that nothing on earth could aid him—and given the state of mental health treatment at the time, he may have been right. There are no records to indicate that Ewan passed a single class at Trinity College.

Ewan had not confided this disturbing aspect of himself to Maud during their courtship, and she later wrote that had she known of his lifelong mental illness, she would never have agreed to the marriage. She maintained that incurable insanity was justification for divorce—though she stood by Ewan, anxious and protective, to the end.

That March, Maud received a strange, troubling post-card from Scotland. It was completely blank, without a single word or image. A few weeks later, Ewan himself arrived back in Prince Edward Island. Ewan stayed away from Maud and avoided Cavendish as he tried, unsuccess-fully at first, to find a new ministry and pull himself back together.

But now Maud had a happy distraction—the happiest of her life. Less than a month after Ewan came home, an acceptance letter arrived from L. C. Page & Company. The letter was dated April 8, 1907. It was signed by the owner and editor, Louis Page himself. They would be delighted to publish *Anne of Green Gables,* he wrote. In fact, as Maud learned much later, it was not Page who had championed her novel but a young visiting intern from Summerside, Prince Edward Island, who had convinced the editors to take a chance on a new author. Maud was beside herself with joy.

L. C. Page & Company offered its first-time author a choice. Maud could accept an outright payment of five hundred dollars—her entire year's income from writing.

Or she could gamble on making a percentage of the earnings, with nothing at all paid in advance.

Maud took the plunge and opted for a royalty instead of the advance. The L. C. Page terms were meager even for the time—offering only 10 percent royalty on the wholesale price of the book. Maud would receive nine cents for each copy sold. The contract also obliged Maud to publish *all* of her books with L. C. Page for the next five years, at this same low "beginner's" rate. She had to commit herself to writing sequels. But Maud balked only at their final condition: Page told the brand-new author to publish under Lucy Maud Montgomery—a name Maud had never liked or used. Eager as she was to publish, Maud held fast. Her books would appear under the name she'd been using all along: L. M. Montgomery.

Maud expected *Anne* to be out that fall, as she jubilantly announced to her pen pals, MacMillan and Weber. But one delay after another kept pushing back the publication date. An early printing contained two garbled sentences and had to be discarded. There were problems with the illustrations, and the artist kept putting off the work. When *Anne of Green Gables* finally appeared in June of 1908, Maud called it an "epoch" in her life, to borrow an expression from Anne.

That precious instant when Maud laid hands on her first published book was a "proud, wonderful, thrilling moment." The book sported a handsome cover and was elegantly bound and printed. The author dedicated this first book to "the memory of my Father and Mother." Grandmother Macneill never received any book dedication, not then, not ever. But Maud told herself how glad her parents would have been, how her father's eyes would have glowed with pride. Maud regarded the volume with the wonder of a new mother, trying not to brag—"Not a great book at all—but mine, mine, mine," she crooned.

The novel's success was immediate and dazzling. *Anne of Green Gables* sold better than Maud could have ever dreamed. Her days were enlivened by the warm reviews that flooded in—almost seventy in all. Maud's novel was universally praised. The book went into a second edition in less than a month, and L. C. Page at once began pressuring their new author for a sequel.

By the end of the year, *Anne of Green Gables* had gone through six editions, and Maud received her first royalty check of $1,730, which meant nearly twenty thousand copies had already sold. "Not bad," she crowed, "for the first six months of a new book by an unknown author!"

Her gamble on herself proved wise. And though she described the novel to Ephraim Weber as "a juvenilish story, ostensibly for girls," she was touched and delighted to discover that it reached so far and deep. Adults embraced the story. Grown men wept over it. She received not only rave reviews, but fan letters from all over the world—some addressed to her as *Mister,* some written directly to *Miss Anne Shirley, Green Gables, Avonlea.* Eager fans offered to tell her their own life stories—to be converted into works of fiction, of course—and one letter, pretending to be from a relative, began, "My dear long-lost uncle."

One fan letter Maud especially treasured came from the seventy-three-year-old Mark Twain—one of her own favorite childhood authors—praising Anne as "the dearest, most lovable child in fiction since the immortal Alice." Maud answered each piece of mail personally, even when eighty-five letters came from Australia on one day.

L. C. Page & Company only published one book that ever outsold *Anne of Green Gables,* the 1913 bestseller *Pollyanna,* which sold more than a million copies in its first year. In both cases, L. C. Page & Company pressed its authors for immediate and numerous sequels. As early as August of 1907, they were demanding a sequel to *Anne of Green Gables.* In October, Maud began writing the first few pages of *Anne of Avonlea,* still full of affection for her central character. But as winter descended, Maud's mood darkened and her enthusiasm flagged.

She confided to MacMillan, "I don't think the book is as good—comparatively speaking—as the first. But I may not be able to judge—I feel so soaked and saturated with 'Anne' that I'm sick of the sound of her name." She was bombarded by requests from fans who flocked to Prince Edward Island hoping to meet her, and "I don't want to be 'met,'" she grumbled.

Along with cold weather came Maud's usual winter depression and fatigue, "coupled with a heavy dread of the future—any future, even a happy one." While she was famous now in the world of children's books, she remained a prisoner at home. She could not leave her aging grandmother for a single day. Nor could she convince her grandmother to make any of the unused rooms in the house as a cozy winter library or study. Instead, with the coming of cold weather, Maud was forced to work in the kitchen, where she was constantly interrupted by the comings and goings of the post office.

That year her nerves also frayed when the kitchen roof caught fire. The day was windy, so the fire spread quickly. Maud dragged a ladder from her uncle John's barn, filled a pail with water, and managed to douse the flames. It was a close call. Maud stayed calm till the danger was over, and then collapsed. All her life, Maud had dreamed of fires. She wondered if those dreams had been prophetic. Now she lived in constant terror that the old homestead would burn to the ground.

Her anxious thoughts turned often toward her upcoming marriage. After his breakdown in Scotland, Ewan took a long time finding his balance again. At first, even his search for a new ministry was unsuccessful. Finally he found a position in the tiny Bloomfield parish, far from Cavendish. Ewan and Maud rarely saw each other. The bride-to-be worried whether, with the strained condition of her nerves, she could possibly be "fit to be his or anyone's wife." She must have also wondered how fit a husband Ewan would prove.

Maud finished that first sequel, *Anne of Avonlea,* in August of 1908, declaring it "not nearly so good as *Green Gables.*" L. C. Page held up the sequel's publication for a time on the grounds that *Anne of Green Gables* was still selling so well that they did not want to compete with their own success.

One early reviewer noted that *Anne of Green Gables* "radiates happiness and optimism." For all its mishaps, pathos, and misadventures, *Anne of Green Gables* is indeed a sort of literary antidepressant. The novel serves as a charm against darkness. The laughter and beauty in the book are never forced, for they came from a deep source. Whatever Maud owed to books like the ever-magical *Alhambra* by Washington Irving she amply repaid in her writings. The brilliant sparkle of her work, its heart-raising effervescence, was hard-earned. "Thank God, I can keep the shadows of my life out of my work," she wrote. "I would not wish to darken any other life — I want instead to be a messenger of optimism and sunshine."

CHAPTER SIXTEEN

"Yes, I Understand the Young Lady Is a Writer"

As Maud's fame increased, Ewan's fortunes slowly rose. He'd become a popular minister at his small parish, and he began once more to turn his attention and ambitions to the wider world. One of Ewan's closest friends, Edwin Smith, had fled Prince Edward Island for the larger scope of the mainland. Smith, a charismatic minister, was thriving off-island. In September 1909, Ewan followed suit and left Prince Edward Island for a double-charge parish in Ontario. There he would wait till Maud was free to marry and join him.

Maud watched Ewan's success with a mixture of pride and horror. Exile from her beloved island home was now inevitable. Ontario was home to Toronto, the literary center of Canada, but it was a far cry from Cavendish—culturally, geographically, and emotionally.

Maud's departure from Cavendish, Prince Edward Island, and all she held dear, weighed heavily on her in the years between the publication of *Anne of Green Gables* and her marriage to Ewan. Though she kept busy writing new books and rereading old favorites, she often felt depressed and worried, and aside from cousin Frede's welcome visits, there was little to distract her. Maud suffered hard days, when she felt "depressed, tired, broken, a prey to indescribable and unconquerable unrest." In 1908 she had a near-total collapse when a cloud of depression seemed to descend, and she could neither eat nor sleep nor work. Ewan's only advice was for Maud to give up writing for a month. She might as easily have promised to give up breathing.

In all likelihood, Maud was in the throes of manic depression. She had always suffered from extreme highs and lows. Now she walked the floor for hours in an agony of nerves. She knew something was seriously wrong, but she refused to consult any local doctors, for fear of gossip. Leaving town—and Grandmother Lucy—was impossible, even for a medical consultation. None of Lucy's five living children took any responsibility for their aging mother. Aunt Emily, less than thirty miles away, had visited just once in three years.

A few years earlier, Uncle John and his son Prescott had broken their chilly silence and come next door to demand once more that eighty-one-year-old Grandmother Macneill move out so that Prescott could marry and move in with his potential bride-to-be. Grandmother would be farmed out to one adult child or another. Maud would be on her own. The suggestion was met with dismay by both women.

The visit turned into a full-blown family feud, with John and Prescott pressing their case, an outraged Maud holding them off, and Grandmother Macneill weeping.

Prescott never married. Instead he fell prey to tuberculosis, the same disease that had killed Maud's mother. Prescott's death hardened Uncle John's heart further against Maud and his mother. He set obstacles in their path at every turn. Maud had to shovel the snow out to the road. She placed buckets beneath more than twenty leaks in the ceiling. Chunks of plaster fell down around her and her aging grandmother.

Despite all this, Maud passionately adored the old homestead. She took long walks in fields and lanes nearby. Lover's Lane sustained her. It was her refuge, an escape from life's trials. She wandered down to the sea at sunset; she strolled in the graveyard where her mother lay buried and where, someday, Maud planned to be buried beside her. On late-night rambles she would spy the old homestead softened by moonlight and realize "how deeply rooted and strong is my love for this old place." It was "terrible," she thought, "to love things—and people—as I do!"

"Smug, opulent Ontario," as she called it, lay ahead in her near future. But Maud's thoughts and dreams carried her back to her past. She began a new children's book that incorporated many of the family tales her great-aunt Mary Lawson told so brilliantly. This new work was called *The Story Girl,* and it became Maud's favorite of all of her books—though she sagely predicted it wouldn't do as well as *Anne of Green Gables.*

The Story Girl cobbles together old family legends and ghost stories with the childhood adventures of a group of fictional Prince Edward Island children. The adventures are linked through tales told by Sara Stanley, the "Story Girl" of the title. ("'I shall learn how to tell stories to all the world,' said the Story Girl dreamily.")

The book's construction allowed Maud free range to play with her own family history and with storytelling as an art: "true things that are, and true things that are not, but might be." The book is set amid the glories of Prince Edward Island, and moments of humor peep constantly through its dreaminess. *The Story Girl* was dedicated to Maud's best friend and cousin Frede, "in remembrance of old days, old dreams, and old laughter"—a favorite book for a favorite friend.

One would never know from reading this jubilant

book how much the author suffered during its composition. Maud lived through dangerous mood swings all that winter and spring, similar in intensity to what she suffered during her ill-fated engagement to Edwin Simpson. In February of 1910 she struggled through a month of "utter prostration—an utter breakdown of body, soul, and spirit." It came on suddenly—Maud was too overwrought to eat or sleep, and as a result she could not work, read, or think straight. She paced the floor, unable to tolerate company but worse when left alone. Maud felt a "morbid dread of the future," though even in her private journals, she never named Ewan or Ontario in that future. She wanted only to die, to rest. She longed for the company of the one person who unfailingly consoled her, her best friend and kindred spirit, cousin Frede. But Frede was away at university, her studies paid for by Maud herself.

Maud started a new novel, *Kilmeny of the Orchard*, based on a story she had attempted earlier. It was her first book-length work about which she expressed serious misgivings. L. C. Page was pressuring her for another novel, and she was not ready to face another book about Anne. Instead, she doubled the length of *Kilmeny of the Orchard*—at that time called *Una of the Garden*—rewriting it all in just a month or two.

Try as she might, Maud was unhappy with the results. She was sure the "padding" her publishers had demanded had weakened the book. She wished she hadn't agreed to allow its publication at all—though later she would defend *Kilmeny* against critical attacks. For the first time, Maud's work received negative reviews. One reviewer called it "a terrible specimen of the American novel of sentiment." Another said that the main character was enough to bring on "a bilious headache."

The first volume of Maud's journal ends on an ominous note that winter of 1910, though at least she was able to work again. She had begun the journal eager and forward-looking. Coming to the last pages gave her the opportunity to read retrospectively.

"They have been in most respects a hard thirteen years," Maud noted. Much had changed in those years—a few things for the better, she hastened to remind herself. She had won her treasured literary recognition, that childhood dream. Perhaps, she mused, she would not have fought quite so hard or climbed so high "lacking the spur of pain."

But still she longed, in her last entry in the journal, on February 7, 1910, for "a little happiness, just for a change."

The year 1910 did in fact bring few happy adventures for Maud. Her work was pulling her out into the world—and sometimes brought the world to her in unexpected ways. Earl Grey, the visiting governor general of Canada, sought *her* out. He was one of the first famous visitors to pay a call to Prince Edward Island on Maud's behalf—but by no means the last. The illustrious visitor sat with

Maud on the steps of a small white building, the two new acquaintances conversing about the surrounding beauty of the place.

What the governor general failed to realize—and Maud knew all too well—was that they were sitting perched on the ladies' outhouse steps. Each time a woman approached, she would spot the two luminaries and hurry away. Maud could barely avoid a fit of hysterical giggles, wondering helplessly if there might be some poor soul trapped inside the outhouse waiting for them to leave.

That fall, Maud set out for her first trip to visit her publisher, L. C. Page & Company in Boston. She stayed at the opulent Brookline home of publisher Louis Page and his wife. The businessman Page had timed things just right. He urged Maud to sign a new contract for *The Story Girl* under the same ungenerous terms as the old contracts. Maud initially resisted.

But finding herself a guest under her publisher's roof, Maud felt she had to agree to renew the old terms. Louis, she wrote, was a "fascinating" character. He wined and dined his visiting author. Maud shopped at the elegant stores of Boston and rode in a motorcar for the first time. She witnessed her first lunar eclipse. She attended lavish parties and was feted, interviewed, and photographed. All this was heady stuff for a girl from a remote Canadian province.

Maud's visit coincided with the twenty-fifth

anniversary of the New England Women's Press Club. More than three hundred members attended, with several of America's leading literary lights present. Maud stood in a receiving line for more than two hours. It was exhausting to thank women over and over for their compliments. Fame, she was discovering, could be hard work, too. But Maud was good at this aspect of being a writer, and a good sport. She was gracious and kind to each fan. The head of the event told Maud gratefully, "You have been our 'great gun' this evening."

An interview appeared in the *Republic* in November 1910 showing the impression Maud made on her new American audience. Though she was thirty-six years old, Maud appeared both younger and more delicate than she was.

> *Miss Montgomery is short and slight, indeed of a form almost childishly small, though graceful and symmetrical. She has an oval face, with delicate aquiline features, bluish-gray eyes and an abundance of dark brown hair. Her pretty pink evening gown . . . accentuated her frail and youthful aspect.*

The *Republic* journalist compared Maud to the countrified young Charlotte Brontë, author of *Jane Eyre,* coming up from Yorkshire to visit London for the first time. Maud, the interviewer decided, must be similarly awestruck. But the Canadian author held her own. Maud's startled interviewer began to see "a determined character, with positive convictions on the advantages of the secluded country life." Maud was unwilling to play the role of the country ingenue; she firmly declined to write Anne's love story and, when pressed, said she knew too little of college life to write about that, either.

Louis Page himself was a fascinating character, but during this visit to Boston, Maud began to seriously distrust him. The young author had had her doubts about L. C. Page & Company for some time. "The feeling is instinctive," she wrote, "and will not down." Maud heard stories about her editor's womanizing, his extravagance and ruthlessness. His way of dealing with female authors revealed a troubling mixture of flirtation and bullying.

Maud regretted that she had allowed herself to be pressed into signing her *Story Girl* contract with its unfair long-term binding clause intact. She began to feel that, both in his business dealings and in his own personal life, Louis Page was not a man to trust. All in all, the visit to Boston was more eye-opening than restful.

As always, Maud's high times were fleeting. In lavish upper-crust Boston, Maud had a taste of the posh life. But back in Cavendish, reality claimed her at once. When she arrived at the train station, her cousin George Campbell picked her up in an old horse and buggy. "Sleet blew into her face the whole way home."

It was rare for Maud to make an extended visit away. Usually she could not leave home even for a day, no matter how short the distance or how pressing the cause. Grandmother Lucy Macneill, now in her late eighties, hated to let her granddaughter out of her sight. It was no use arguing. "One might as well talk to a pillar of granite." When a poem of Maud's was set to music and performed at the opera house in nearby Charlottetown, Maud missed the performance—and her own curtain call. As she wrote to pen pal Ephraim Weber, "The author couldn't go. She had to stay home and wish she could."

In February of 1911, Maud was forced to travel into town to take care of a bad tooth. As she was leaving, her grandmother hobbled outside to say good-bye. "It struck me how very frail and old grandmother looked. She had dressed hurriedly and was consequently rather untidy. . . . But apart from that there was a look in her face that sent a chill to my heart." All her life, Maud had experienced strange foretelling dreams and uncanny intuitions. She feared this was another such moment.

Her premonition was so strong that Maud nearly sent the horses away. She rode to Charlottetown haunted by the look she had seen in the gray morning light. After her appointment, the Charlottetown Women's Club threw a reception in Maud's honor, but she was worried and distracted and hurried home over sleety roads only to find her grandmother "quite well and smiling" by a snug fire with her favorite cat, Daffy. Maud dismissed her own fears as foolishness.

Less than two weeks later, Maud and her grandmother both came down with the flu. They were improving by early March, and their good friend Tillie McKenzie Houston came to pay a sympathy call. That night Maud cried herself to sleep. Once again she was haunted by a paralyzing dread. She kept murmuring over and over a line from Edgar Allan Poe: "At nightfall the tired body and dull brain went back to their rest."

As it turned out, that night would be the last she ever spent in her upstairs childhood sanctuary, her "white and peaceful nest." The next day, Grandmother Macneill took a sudden turn for the worse, and Maud didn't leave her side for several days. She slept downstairs, near her grandmother. They moved a bed into the sitting room, settling Grandmother Macneill close to the fireplace. The doctor came—despite Grandmother's protests—and gravely informed Maud that the old lady had pneumonia. At her age, such a serious illness "could have but one ending." Friends and neighbors paid their last respects. Even grim Uncle John trudged next door for the first time in five years, to say good-bye to his dying mother. Maud watched him stumble away "with laggard step and bowed head like an old man."

Lucy Macneill passed away as quietly and uncomplainingly as she had lived. Maud had observed her grandmother fold her hands after doing the dishes, a gesture that struck her with its finality, folding them "forever after the work of almost eighty-seven years." In death, those knotted, work-worn hands underwent a miraculous transformation. They looked "beautiful again in the consecration of death." Her smile seemed to Maud both radiant and wise.

But nothing else held still after Grandmother's death. Maud was ordered out of the house immediately. She could stay just long enough to pack her things. For the first time in her life, she was literally homeless.

Uncle John's heart had softened enough to allow a final visit to his dying mother, but once the house was legally his, he turned his back on it forever. Rather than allow Maud to go on living there, he let the old homestead stand empty, then crumble into ruins before he finally tore it down in 1920.

The Cavendish townsfolk put together a hasty farewell ceremony for Maud, as simple as it was heartfelt. Maud donated the farmhouse organ to the church whose yard housed her mother's grave. Maud left Cavendish on a cold, windy day, closing the door of the old house behind her.

She wrote,

All the bitterness of death was in that moment—and

it was repeated as we drove up through Cavendish and familiar scenes and beloved haunts disappeared one by one from view—the manse, the old trees that encircled home, the graveyard on the hill with its new red mound, the woods in which was Lover's Lane—beautiful, unforgotten, unforgettable Lover's Lane—the sea-shore, the pond, the houses of friends—all drifted finally out of sight. I had left Cavendish forever, save as a fitful visitor; and in leaving it felt that I was leaving the only place on earth my heart would ever truly love.

Maud spent a few months at Park Corner, trying to recover and putting together her long-delayed wedding trousseau. Maud was still mourning Grandmother Lucy, whose absence in her life seemed "an impossible—an outrageous thing. . . . She had always been there." That simple line—*She had always been there*—was as close to a loving eulogy as Maud could ever manage. Grandmother Lucy Macneill meant home, and with her death, Maud lost her essential touchstone.

The future was rushing upon her. Ewan Macdonald had waited patiently for his bride for five years. Maud finally told her pen pal George MacMillan, "I expect to be married to the Rev. Mr. Macdonald." MacMillan and Ewan had met years earlier while Ewan was in Scotland.

Maud felt happy that MacMillan approved of her friend—without giving any clue at the time that the young minister was more than a casual acquaintance.

She had expressed herself to MacMillan numerous times on the idea of marriage, and in these letters, one sees her paving the way to her own. She proposed that "for friendship there should be similarity; but for love there must be dissimilarity." She and Herman had been very different—or so Maud maintained. Herman was quiet; Maud was a chatterbox. He was a simple farmer; she had higher ambitions. She saw herself as an intellectual, and Herman was not interested in ideas. Yet she had adored and desired him.

She told MacMillan—while secretly engaged—"If two people have a mutual affection for each other, don't bore each other, and are reasonably well mated in point of age and social position . . . their prospects of happiness together would be excellent." Such a sensible match might lack the "highest upflashings" of the divine spark, she admitted, but added that if she ever did marry, "that is the base on which I shall found my marriage."

By summer of 1911, Maud no longer needed a husband in order to survive. She had earned financial independence and an international reputation. Her books were still selling well; she was, by any standard of the time, a wealthy woman. She could have afforded to buy a house of her own and to maintain it.

She also had one last chance at that spark of passion and romance that year. With Ewan far away in Leaskdale, Ontario, Maud's dashing cousin Oliver Macneill came to town and began to court her with determination and vigor. Oliver Macneill was a wealthy man. He was a handsome divorcé who, according to Maud's journal, kindled that "devastating flame of the senses." She felt drawn to him against her will, much as she'd been to Herman Leard.

Oliver Macneill asked Maud to marry him — in fact, he offered her every kind of unorthodox arrangement. She could marry him for just a year and then be rid of him; she could live independently if she liked. Maud found herself teetering once more on a tempting precipice. But in the end, her feeling of loyalty and commitment to Ewan Macdonald won out. She sent Oliver packing, and vowed to "walk in Lover's Lane with him no more."

None of this kept her moods from vacillating in those months leading up to the wedding. She was mourning her grandmother, her Cavendish friends, and her lost, never-to-be-forgotten home by the sea. She was tormented by memories of Lover's Lane. "Not a day passes that I do not think of it."

And Maud was needled by yet another secret grief: her friend Tillie's husband, Will Houston, had declared his passion for Maud shortly before Tillie's death. Maud had been shocked and horrified. To her, Will and Tillie seemed

211

an ideal couple and were two of her closest friends. Already tremulous on the eve of her marriage, this revelation made her even more anxious.

Luckily, Maud was at merry Park Corner, "the wonder castle of my childhood," surrounded by those who knew and loved her best. She spent hours discussing life and literature with her cousin Bertie. The house was full of happy memories. Here at the turn of the staircase was that place on the wall where they had measured their changing height, year after year.

Her relatives at Park Corner were delighted by the arrival of Maud's elegant trousseau. Maud had ordered clothing from Montreal—likely with cousin Frede's advice. Maud pasted swatches of trousseau fabrics into her scrapbook: violet silk with lace trim, sprigged floral print with lilac pansies against a cream background. A cocoa-brown muslin and a black evening dress. Maud had worn black all that spring in mourning for her grandmother, but now she laid it aside with relief. Maud wrote, "Color is to me what music is to some. Everybody likes color; with me it is a passion."

In mid-June, Frede came home to Park Corner from Montreal for a joyful reunion. Together the cousins traveled to Cavendish—an easier visit home than Maud had anticipated. "It was all a sweet pleasure to be there again in that June beauty." Cavendish, it seemed, could never lose its capacity to refresh and delight her.

On Tuesday, July 4, 1911, the evening before the wedding, Ewan, the bridegroom himself, arrived from Ontario. That night, Maud did two things she had never expected to do on the eve of her wedding—she cried a little and then "slept soundly the rest of the night!" Why did she cry? she wondered. She was "content," the bland word she used over and over regarding this marriage. The blandness hid a deeper loss: "I think I wept a lost dream—a dream that could never be fulfilled—a girl's dream of the lover who should be her perfect mate, to whom she might splendidly give herself with no reservations. We all dream that dream. And when we surrender it unfulfilled we feel that something wild and sweet and unutterable has gone out of life!"

Maud's wedding day dawned cool and gray, promising rain. Maud wore a simple, soft-looking dress of ivory and silk crepe with touches of chiffon. There is no photograph of her wearing the gown, though the dress still survives, and a replica stands on display at her birthplace museum. From a modern perspective, Maud's wedding gown is a simple day dress with soft ruffles around the neck and hem. Examined more closely, one sees the gleam of pearl beading on the tunic. The most eccentric part of her wedding trousseau was an elaborate, high hat trimmed with all kinds of flowers. Maud posed with the hat in several photos, and it makes her look a foot taller at least.

The wedding took place at noon in the front parlor

of the Park Corner house. Maud's friend and cousin Ella Campbell played on the organ "The Voice That Breathed O'er Eden" as the bride came downstairs on her uncle John Campbell's arm. She carried a bouquet of white flowers—roses and lilies of the valley—and ferns. Around her neck she wore Ewan's wedding gift, a pearl and amethyst necklace. She felt surprisingly calm.

We know nothing about Ewan's state of mind; in her descriptions of the wedding and the honeymoon, Maud barely mentions him. Very little of Ewan's voice comes down to us in his own words. We know that he is supposed to have said drily, in response to some friend's remark about Maud's fame, "Yes, I understand the young lady is a writer." The line, uttered before their marriage, sounds apologetic, as if he had learned that his fiancée collected oddities, and hoped she might outgrow it.

Theirs was not the ideal wedding Maud had once imagined—she dreamed of an elopement deep in the woods, with trees forming a green cathedral overhead, and the two lovers declaring their vows in solitude. But the new bride declared herself, again, "content" with her simple ceremony.

Cousin Frede concocted an elaborate wedding feast after the service. The instant Maud sat down to that wedding dinner, she "felt a sudden horrible inrush of rebellion and despair." Reality hit swiftly and hard. Maud resisted a mad urge to tug off the wedding ring and run away. Instead she sat shrouded in her white veil, "a helpless prisoner," staring down at her plate, "as unhappy as I have ever been in my life." She could not eat a bite of Frede's splendid dinner.

On their departure from Park Corner, the wedding party found itself riding behind a hearse. They traveled as if part of the large funeral, mile after mile. Maud tried to laugh it off at the time, but later she came to think of it as a forbidding omen.

CHAPTER SEVENTEEN

"Those Whom the Gods Wish to Destroy"

Maud barely mentions Ewan during their honeymoon, either in her journal or in long letters home. In a photograph taken on board ship during their honeymoon, Ewan Macdonald stands out from the other passengers. He looks taller, handsomer, slimmer, and more masculine, perhaps granted a few extra inches in height by his tall black minister's hat. Still, he seems very much at the center of things, as one always imagines Maud to have been. He is turned slightly to face the others, and one can see his dimpled smile.

Maud's book royalties paid for the honeymoon. The couple spent the first three months of their married life traveling through England and Scotland, a journey that had long been one of Maud's dreams, to visit the Old Country. Maud's initial reaction to Europe was characteristic. She felt "homesick—suddenly, wretchedly, unmitigatedly homesick!"

Maud kept comparing England—unfavorably—with Prince Edward Island. But at one castle she spied some unusual small blue flowers that had grown all over her grandmother's yard in Cavendish. Surely, she marveled, Grandmother Lucy Macneill, who had been born and raised in England, brought those blue flowers to Canada and planted them in remembrance of her lost home.

England sparked other family connections, too. Maud had never forgotten the magical green-spotted china dogs from Grandfather Montgomery's house in Park Corner— the ceramic dogs her father claimed had leaped onto the hearthrug at midnight. In England she found two pairs. The larger pair had gold spots and were so huge they wouldn't fit on a mantelpiece; she decided these precious souvenirs would guard the hearth at their new manse. She bought both pairs and shipped them home.

Maud had arranged to meet her longtime pen pal George MacMillan in Scotland. There he would join them on their travels. It was an odd arrangement for a honeymoon, made even more awkward by the fact that MacMillan brought along his fiancée, an attractive young woman named Miss Jean Allen. Miss Allen, at age twenty, was by far the youngest member of the foursome. She was, according to Maud, a "very pretty girl," with bright gold hair and a "simply exquisite" complexion. But she proved cranky and hard to please. Her personality was less dazzling than her looks, Maud quickly decided, noting Miss Allen's only "stock in trade is her twenty-year-old freshness and charming complexion."

Maud did not recognize her Scottish pen pal on sight. It was Ewan and MacMillan who spotted each other from their meeting years earlier in Glasgow. George MacMillan was a "slight, fair, nice-looking chap," she wrote. Maud warmed to him at once. Years later she would joke about marrying MacMillan off to her dear cousin Bertie McIntyre. But most important, he was "one of the best conversationalists I have ever met." When the four went off on excursions, Maud and MacMillan spent all their time in conversation while the lovely Miss Allen sulked and seethed.

Ewan mildly pointed out that Miss Allen probably felt left out while Maud and MacMillan were busily "absorbed in long literary discussions." From then on, Maud made a point to walk with either Miss Allen or with Ewan, but nothing improved Miss Allen's mood. She tried to prevent a rowing expedition, and when that failed, she stormed off alone. In the end, MacMillan did not marry the irritable Miss Allen but remained a bachelor all his life.

The newlyweds traveled on alone through the British

Isles. They didn't visit the Isle of Skye, the ancestral home of Ewan's family. Nor did Maud seek out her own living Scottish relations. Instead they conducted a literary tour of Scotland, places connected with her favorite Scottish authors — Sir Walter Scott, the poet Robert Burns, and J. M. Barrie. The Scottish sky, she wrote, was nearly beautiful enough to make up for the absence of the sea.

The names on the shops gave Maud a "nice 'at home' feeling," she said — all those Simpsons and Macneills. One day she and Ewan found a stand of spruce trees and pulled their own chew of the bittersweet gum. But the Old Country did not live up to her imagined ideal — nothing could. Prince Street in Edinburgh was not the street "of my dreams — the fairy avenue of gardens and statuary and palaces."

It is easy to guess that this was not the honeymoon of her dreams, either, though Maud did not write about the intimate details of those first nights with her husband. Clearly, the "Mad Passion" was missing. Nor was Ewan a deeply kindred spirit. We know that Maud suffered from painful cystitis, known as the "honeymoon disease," so it's likely that she and Ewan were sexually active. But theirs was, from the start, a marriage of companionship rather than a meshing of souls.

Maud's favorite romantic moment was sitting with Ewan at the edge of a quiet forest after they had parted ways from George MacMillan and Miss Allen. This was closer to her ideal, sitting in a wood overlooking the lake, apart from rest of the busy world, "in a little bit of 'honeymooning' in our green seclusion."

One of the last stops was Dunwich, England, where Grandmother Macneill had lived till the age of twelve. Maud had expected to feel a mild interest in the place, but she was shocked by the depth of her response. "My emotion almost overpowered me. It seemed to me that grandmother and Aunt Margaret must be somewhere around, little laughing girls of twelve and fourteen . . . I was homesick—and yet I felt as if I had come home."

After ten weeks away, Ewan and Maud were ready to begin their new lives in Ontario. Maud had made arrangements for work to be done at the manse in their absence. Sailing in September through rougher seas than on the outward-bound journey, she felt eager to "build my nest and gather my scattered household gods all about me." For the first time in her life, Maud had a home of her own.

They arrived September 24, 1911, on a "damp murky autumn night," and drove the seven miles home in darkness. It turned out that the manse was far from ready—it wasn't even habitable. Other housing arrangements had to be made, and quickly. Ewan and Maud boarded with Mary and Lizzie Oxtoby, two elderly, eccentric spinster sisters "who would have delighted Dickens," Maud wrote.

They did not delight Maud. The two old women were extremely curious about the new minister and his

wife, and pried into their every move. The Macdonalds'
temporary bedroom was tiny and inconvenient, and the
Oxtoby sisters were poor cooks. Lizzie Oxtoby laughed
at everything. Maud declared that if you told Lizzie your
father had hanged himself, your husband had gone mad,
and your children burned to death, Lizzie still would have
chuckled.

The village of Leaskdale was practically nonexistent,
a mere ten or twelve houses in all. The Macdonalds lived
near the blacksmith and the wheelwright. The manse,
Maud wrote, was an "ugly L-shaped" pale brick, a style
popular at the time in Ontario. Unfortunately for the large
china dogs, the house did not have a hearth at all. Maud
named the dogs Gog and Magog, after two fierce Biblical
characters, and installed them on either side of her bookcase. The manse didn't have an indoor bathroom or toilet,
much to Maud's dismay. But it was spacious, with room to
grow: five bedrooms, a parlor, a dining room, a kitchen,
and a library.

In one of the most touching scenes in Maud's later
novel *Anne's House of Dreams,* Anne Shirley tears herself from her cozy seaside house of dreams and moves
to a large house in town, close to where her husband,
Gilbert, works. Anne's housemaid Susan praises the new
house as such "'a fine, big one.' 'I hate big houses,' sobbed
Anne."

Maud was living out this same scene. She mourned her

lost Cavendish and Prince Edward Island. But she quickly charged in and took hold. As the minister's wife, Maud found herself at the center of things. Though she initially wrote of Leaskdale, "There isn't one interesting or really intelligent person in it," she soon grew attached to the people and landscape. Some of her most peaceful years were spent in Leaskdale, creating community and family.

Ewan's ministry was a double charge, with one church and the manse in Leaskdale, and the second church in Zephyr, about eleven miles away. Of the two, Maud much preferred Leaskdale. Zephyr's church was older, unattractive, and dimly lit. The people in Zephyr were poorer and less gracious. The road there was dangerous, often muddy and full of ruts. And because Zephyr was also home to a Methodist church, there were rancorous divisions in town that even the gentle Ewan could not smooth over.

The Leaskdale congregation held mostly well-to-do farmers. The day after the Macdonalds' arrival, the church was packed, partly out of eagerness to hear the new minister, partly to greet his famous wife, the acclaimed author of *Anne of Green Gables.*

A few days later, John Mustard's brother, of all people — it seemed she never could escape the Mustards — officiated at Ewan's welcoming ceremony. By the oddest coincidence, Maud noted, she had "come to live in John Mustard's old home." John Mustard was now a distinguished minister in nearby Toronto, married and with a family. He was much admired, if not by Maud, then by the rest of the world.

The Leaskdale manse would never be entirely Maud's own house, of course—it belonged to the church—but she could make it as beautiful as she pleased. She had the resources, the energy, and, for the first time in her life, no one to stand in her way. Maud was so eager to begin that the Macdonalds moved in before the manse was fully ready. Maud had the floors painted green instead of the usual gray. She put up her favorite fern-patterned wallpaper. In the library, shared with Ewan, she finally had room enough for all of her books.

Here they hung framed photographs of favorite places on Prince Edward Island, as well as copies of the paintings from her three book covers: *Anne of Green Gables, Kilmeny of the Orchard,* and *The Story Girl.* Their bedroom featured pearl-gray furniture and a bright red rug. Maud painted one bedroom pink and white, another bright blue. She created a sewing room on the landing, and a fourth and fifth bedroom were set up for storage and a maid's quarters, respectively. In the parlor with the spotted china dogs, Maud proudly displayed her great-grandmother's enormous heirloom jug, known simply as the Woolner jug. It made a handy conversation piece for visitors and guests.

The house was prettily situated with a lovely lawn and room for a garden. Behind the manse lay a lane that reminded Maud of her much-loved and forever-missed

Lover's Lane. She would go there for long walks whenever she could manage a spare hour for herself.

Before their marriage, Ewan had told his friends, "Yes, I understand the young lady is a writer," but he assumed his wife's life would be dedicated to his work, his happiness. After the marriage, Ewan tried to persuade Maud to publish under Mrs. Macdonald. Maud refused. There is no evidence that Ewan was a fan of Maud's work. She later wrote, perhaps unfairly, that she wasn't sure he'd ever read a single word she had written. She never dedicated a book to her husband.

As a minister's wife, Maud lived in the public eye, always on call. She was in charge of keeping the household in order—the cooking, the cleaning, the washing, the ironing. She attended countless social and church events, and was regularly "at home" to the members of her husband's congregation. This meant hours of visits filled with idle chat. Maud wished she could spend more time on her own, writing. She desperately missed her solitude. She wrote in exasperation to George MacMillan, "Those whom the gods wish to destroy they make ministers' wives."

Thanks to her writing income, the Macdonalds could afford household help. Maud insisted that the servants eat in the dining room with the family. Indeed, some of her closest relationships were with these helpers. Maud planned out meals and chores a week in advance, and each day had its particular tasks and menus. Maud prided herself on being a good cook and housekeeper. She loved to garden. Her handiwork in sewing and embroideries survives, in monograms and floral flourishes, elegant and accomplished. All in all, she found these early days in the new Leaskdale manse a busy and "exciting time."

Maud also involved herself in the life of the congregation. Like her great-aunt Mary Lawson, she was a great storyteller, with a quick and ready wit. Her first "at homes" took place just a few days after she moved into the manse, and "thereafter on the afternoon and evening of Tuesday each week."

Maud managed to make time for her own work—writing drafts by hand in the morning and typing in the afternoon. Then, tired though she might be, she must "dress and go out to tea in the evening 'making small talk,'" taking care not to slight or neglect a soul. Sometimes she could barely keep her eyes open. Those unending pastoral visits, she declared, were "an invention of the devil himself."

She also had church work waiting each time she visited the smaller, poorer church in Zephyr. Maud came to dread the eleven-mile journey there, with an icy wind sleeting across their faces in winter and an equally chilly welcome from the congregation. No matter where she and Ewan went to call for tea, they were always served the same dismal fare: cold pork and fried potatoes. She began to call the Thursdays on which she had to travel to Zephyr "Black Thursdays."

She infinitely preferred her time with the youth group in Leaskdale. Maud enjoyed the company of young people, and the "young fry" admired Maud's energy and good humor. Maud had a reputation for "making things go." Soon she was organizing the kind of evenings of recitations, lively discussions, and entertainment she herself had craved as a girl. She joined the local reading club and taught a Sunday-school class at her husband's church. More requests poured in from nearby communities, but Maud firmly turned down invitations elsewhere.

Her own writing was, she confided to her journal, "as truly 'given' to me as any missionary's or minister's." Ewan would have been appalled by this declaration. He came to learn, often to his distress, that nothing on earth—not her duties as a minister's wife, as a mother, or as a church member—would keep L. M. Montgomery from writing. Maud was well practiced in leading a double life; she had been doing it forever. Her imagined worlds and characters were as real to her as those around her. She "shut the door of [her] soul" to distractions and retreated "into a citadel of dear thoughts and beautiful imaginings."

After that first year, Maud wrote to George MacMillan, "I like Leaskdale very much . . . I do not love it." She tried to be tactful and kind, understanding her peculiar power and status as minister's wife. She got along with most of the congregants. Still, she wrote, the inner "gates of my soul are barred against them. They do not have the key." She'd have gladly exchanged all the scenery in Ontario, she declared, for one walk in Lover's Lane at sunset.

Maud suffered no winter depression that first year, despite — or perhaps because of — the busyness of her days. She managed to write steadily, working on two new story collections. In October 1911, Maud wrote in her journal: "I am contented — I may say happy. There is an absolute happiness and a comparative happiness. Mine is the latter. After the unhappiness and worry of the past thirteen years this existence of mine seems to me a very happy one. I am — for the most part — content."

Soon contentment turned to joy. At age thirty-seven, Maud worried that she had waited too long to have children. In November, she learned she was pregnant. The news filled her with elation. It seemed "so incredible — so wonderful — so utterly impossible as happening to me!"

In celebration, Maud took the final step toward making their house a home. She sent back to Prince Edward Island for her cat, Daffy, the sleek, aloof pet that even cat-hating Grandmother Macneill had loved. He was shipped in a wooden crate from Cavendish, and when the Macdonalds' neighbors rode in with the precious cargo, they warned Maud to expect the worst. Not a sound came from inside the box. Poor Maud was sure that her cat was dead. She pried open the crate. Daffy daintily stepped out and kissed her—a rare display of affection—and then showed his dislike for travel by vanishing for the rest of the day.

Maud always kept at least one pet cat around. Even when she traveled, she took photographs of local cats. "The only true animal is a cat, and the only true cat is a gray cat," she once declared. She owned many cats in her lifetime, mostly gray ones, but striped cats and tabbies and black kittens made their way into her life as well. She autographed her books with a characteristic black cat drawn underneath her signature. Daffy was especially dear because of his connection to Prince Edward Island—"the only living link between me and the old life," she wrote.

Maud had always been thin, and never especially strong. She worried about her ability to see this first pregnancy to term. Cousin Frede traveled to Leaskdale to be with Maud for the birth. Maud hired a professional nurse instead of using a midwife and arranged for a doctor to attend the birth as well.

Toward the end of her pregnancy, Maud had a frightening dream. In it, a black coffin was laid across her feet. She feared it meant that she or her child, or both, would die in childbirth. In 1912, this was not an unreasonable fear—infant and maternal mortality rates were high. Much later in her life, she would look back to that dark foreboding dream: her first son, the open coffin weighing her down. Her griefs and worries over this much-desired, cherished firstborn boy would one day prove nearly fatal indeed.

Chester Cameron Macdonald was born a little after noon on July 7, 1912, a healthy baby boy. It was an easy birth. The wonderful Frede was at Maud's side—another blessing. What's more, her cherished cousin stayed on to help with the new baby. Maud and Frede worked "in beautiful concord," Maud noted, adding that she had at long last "the home I had dreamed of having." The two women adored little "Punch," as they nicknamed him. Chester was an easy baby that first year.

Maud and Frede delighted in all of Chester's treasured firsts. His first word was "Wow!" Together they made up silly poems about him. Ewan was a proud father, but he left the daily rearing, the discipline, even the religious education of children to Maud. Her adoration for this newborn son "blent and twined with the inmost fibres of my being." Maud grieved over each event that marked her firstborn's growing up and away from her. She mourned when they shortened Chester's long nightgowns, sighed over his first cup of milk, and cried the day he was weaned. But "motherhood is heaven," she marveled. "It pays for all."

Maud never stopped writing—not through pregnancy, nor after giving birth. She woke early, around six a.m., and wrote by hand a few hours each morning. She typed during the afternoon—a long, hard task, but her handwriting was so bad she feared no one else could decode it. There were now book-related business matters to manage as well—fan mail, personal correspondence, and money matters to attend to, in addition to all her household duties as minister's wife and new mother. Evenings she reserved for reading, staying up late into the night.

Maud stayed astonishingly productive all through early motherhood, publishing almost a book a year. The year Chester was born, Maud published a collection of stories, *Chronicles of Avonlea*. She had sent L. C. Page & Company several stories to choose from, assuming they would discard the rest. But Page not only retyped and kept all those stories; the publisher would later insist on claiming the work as their own property.

In 1913, Maud published the sequel to *The Story Girl*, titled *The Golden Road*. As always, Maud fretted that the sequel was not as strong as her first book. She was relieved when critics and fans disagreed.

Maud's troubles during these early years in Leaskdale were chiefly comic rather than serious. When Frede visited Leaskdale she brought along her thorny older sister, Stella. Stella was unmarried and at loose ends. She stayed on as a salaried maid for the Macdonalds, though by all accounts she tyrannized the household. Ewan especially disliked and feared her sharp tongue. Stella was bossy, quarrelsome, and a hypochondriac—and she seemed ready to stay put in Leaskdale forever. In many ways, she represented the worst of all the family habits and temperament—with Grandfather Macneill's prickly temper and Grandmother Macneill's dislike and resentment of company. But Stella was family. It was impossible to simply dismiss her or ask her to leave.

If fierce, Stella was also fiercely loyal. If hard-driving, she would nonetheless "work her fingers to the bone for you, complaining bitterly" every minute. She chided Maud in front of guests for not putting enough cream in the company's tea, and when Maud was asked when she planned to begin spring cleaning, Stella interrupted to say, "*I* am going to begin next week." Frede was finally able to convince her older sister she was needed back at home in Park Corner. The Macdonalds heaved a sigh of relief and hired a new maid named Lily, who proved more tractable.

Frede stayed on in Leaskdale, helping with baby Chester till December, then left for a teaching post in Alberta. Her departure left a gaping hole in Maud's domestic and personal life. Without Frede, Maud had "no real friend near." The cousins had confided in each other, gossiped, sat in companionable silence, or talked philosophy. Maud and Frede had secretly conducted séances together over a Ouija board—till rumor got out that the minister's wife was seen trying to summon the devil.

Maud delighted in her newfangled Victrola, but she

and Frede had to turn the volume down low so the neighbors wouldn't hear. Without Frede's company, Maud felt bereft. "I have no social life here . . . not even as much as I had in Cavendish," she mourned.

Of course, Maud had the company of her husband and beloved infant son. But nothing replaced the merriment, intimacy, and ease she felt with Frede. It's hard to gauge Ewan's role in his wife's life, since Maud wrote so little directly about her marriage. Her silence on the subject speaks volumes. We know that one Valentine's Day he called her "the dearest little wife in the world," and that such open expressions of affection were rare. Ewan was a shy, reserved, and reticent man—the opposite of what Maud always craved.

Superficially, they had seemed well matched. Both were Presbyterian, educated; both were of a certain class. But Ewan's humor leaned toward practical jokes. He was so slow-moving and soft-spoken that he struck strangers as dull, while Maud was all mercurial brilliance and shimmer. Ewan was at ease only when speaking off the cuff in public, just where Maud was tongue-tied. Ewan was melancholy at heart, while Maud loved merriment. Perhaps in the end they were not different enough to be lovers, nor kindred enough to be friends.

In those early years, Maud as a lark took one of the quizzes that still appear today in popular magazines. She copied her answers into her journal. Her favorite time of day was sunset and the hour just following. Her favorite season, spring. But when it came to her "idea of happiness," she hesitated. First she wrote flippantly, "a good novel and a plate of russet apples." Next she thought of her darling son, Chester. "But to be in the arms of a man whom I loved with all my heart . . . is, after all, every woman's real idea of happiness, if she would be honest enough to admit it. There are dear and sweet minor happinesses. But that is the only perfect one."

Maud lacked perfect happiness, undoubtedly. Her marriage to Ewan often left her lonely. Yet life still brimmed with "dear and sweet" moments. In 1913 she set to work at last on *Anne of the Island,* the romantic college novel her Boston interviewer had urged her to write years earlier. Maud was reluctant to begin this sequel in Anne's story, and the work went slowly.

Maud always disliked the first stage of planning a book. Once the writing began in earnest, it became a challenge *not* to write. She was known among her friends and relations for talking to herself, trying out lines from her novel, and then rushing out of a room to set them down. She'd laugh out loud when a funny scene came to her. But she had difficulty re-entering the "atmosphere of Anne — like putting on a dress worn years ago . . . something I have outgrown." Her publisher pressured her to produce more and more Anne books, as did her fans.

Though she struggled to find entry into the novel, *Anne of the Island* is one of Montgomery's most beautiful and fully imagined books. It is filled with a host of memorable secondary characters that were always Maud's great stock in trade. It may be second only to *Anne of Green Gables* in its lyricism and accomplishment. *Anne of the Island* features an unforgettable death scene, based on what Maud had witnessed in the early death of her close childhood friend and relation, Penzie Macneill. But it's also a story full of the promise of youth. Maud would question the value of *Anne of the Island,* published during the first dark days of World War I, but critics and readers have always loved it.

That same summer, Maud returned to Prince Edward Island, the place she still called "home." Her first glimpse of the ever-present blue shimmering sea from the crest of a red hill struck her to the heart. At that moment, she confided to George MacMillan, "it seemed passionately to me that I could never leave it again."

Maud did not visit the old Macneill homestead on this trip back, but she stayed nearby for nearly three weeks, "beautiful weeks, with a vein of sadness running through them." She went down to the shore and indulged in reviving "dips" in the sea. She, baby Chester, and Ewan wandered through fields of oxeye daisies and drove over the red island roads. Maud picked wild strawberries and strolled among the fir trees in dew-dampened air till it seemed as if she had "never been away from Cavendish and as if my Ontario home was a dream."

The old Macneill household had been neglected and boarded up by Maud's uncle John, and Maud could not bring herself to go near it. Instead she walked in Lover's Lane; in fact, she "haunted it by day and night." Finally, one evening at dusk, Maud climbed a hill overlooking her old house and gazed down at her own familiar window, and the orchard, woods, and lanes. It all looked the same and, at the same time, utterly changed—precious and unreachable as her dream of married love. "And I went back from that pilgrimage . . . with a very full heart."

Maud soon learned she was pregnant again. This time she hoped for a little girl. She was at work on *Anne of the Island,* and once returned to Leaskdale, she felt amazed to find herself "glad to be back—to be home!"

The year 1913 began full of promise. Ewan had started a foreign missionary program through the Leaskdale church. A successful missionary program often served as a stepping-stone to more prestigious congregations. Maud and Ewan had their eye on the large, elegant city of Toronto. Maud often visited Toronto when she wanted contact with the Canadian literary world.

And she was developing a lucrative second career as a popular public speaker. In October, she addressed a crowd of nearly one thousand women at the Women's Canadian

Club in Toronto. She went not as Mrs. Macdonald, the minister's wife, but as L. M. Montgomery. Both Maud and Ewan felt renewed, energetic, and hopeful about their future. They had no way to guess at the storms that lay just ahead.

CHAPTER EIGHTEEN

A Changed World

Maud's second pregnancy proved harder than her first. She suffered constant nausea and exhaustion, and spent a miserable last few days in 1913 trying to survive the holidays. She confided to her journal that she would be "bitterly disappointed if the baby is not a girl." Maud was nearing forty, and believed this second baby would be her last. She felt more anxious about this birth than the first, with neither cousins Stella nor Frede nearby to help or ease her loneliness.

On August 13, 1914, Maud's worst fears proved real. Her second son—named Hugh Alexander after her father and maternal grandfather—was delivered stillborn, the umbilical cord knotted around his neck. By the time Maud was fully awake, the beautiful baby lay dead beside her. "Little Hugh," as she called him, was buried in Zion Cemetery, near Uxbridge. Maud's grief over the lost child was intense, her heartbreak mingled with guilt. If only she had not wished for a girl! The doctor assured her that infant deaths were common; Maud was not to blame. Still she suffered a long, slow, sad convalescence. She wrote to George MacMillan, "All the sorrow of my life before put together could not equal it in agony." Only the company of baby Chester, sweet-tempered and affectionate, brought Maud any solace.

The world was swept up in its own turmoil. On June 28, 1914, the Archduke Franz Ferdinand of Austria was assassinated in the small, little-known country of Serbia. This was the first match lit in the firestorm later known as World War I. On August 5, Maud noted with horror that England had declared war on Germany. She could not believe it—it seemed to her "a horrible dream." Less than two weeks later, her baby lay buried in Zion Cemetery, and terrifying war news continued to spread. "Civilization," wrote Maud, "stands aghast at the horror that is coming upon it."

Most of Maud's well-to-do farmer neighbors in Leaskdale felt aloof from the war in Europe. Maud's passionate involvement was unusual for her place and time. She became president of the local Red Cross and later traveled around, "stumping" for conscription—a mandatory draft for Canadians.

Maud followed the war news as if her life depended every skirmish. Again, little Chester was her comfort in the face of grief and anxiety. One night she took him into her own bed, and in the middle of the night, she felt him kissing her hand. In her diary she wrote, "What a blessing you are to me! Will you always be so?" When she thought of the soldiers dying in foreign fields and of children murdered in Belgium, she pictured her own son.

She told George MacMillan, only half jokingly, that she had "not had one decent dinner since the war began." The mail arrived each day at twelve thirty, a half hour before lunch. If the news was good, Maud felt too excited to eat. If bad, she was too distraught.

To her neighbors, Maud's fixation on the war news seemed crazy. She took some comfort in writing to MacMillan, who was living in Scotland, in the thick of things. But she worried constantly that zeppelins were falling on him. She began to dream about battles, and many of the dreams struck her as ominous. According to her own count, she had more than ten predictive dreams during the course of the war.

Maud was still at work on her college novel, *Anne of the Island*. She felt ridiculous writing about college parties, exams, and romances while the world was falling to pieces. But as she had promised herself years earlier, she meant to be a "messenger of optimism and sunshine." Maud's writing would later be given to Polish soldiers during World

War II, to comfort and strengthen them. The book they chose was another novel Maud composed during the first world war, *Anne's House of Dreams*.

Maud turned forty in 1914, and she remained full of hopes, dreams, and ambitions. She learned to her great joy that she was pregnant a third time. Bad news followed on the heels of the good. A letter came from Montreal, warning that her precious cousin Frede was dangerously ill with typhoid fever. Doctors feared the worst, and Maud panicked. She "could not face a world with no Frede in it." The two friends had shared every confidence since the long, hot summer night in Park Corner when they first discovered each other as kindred spirits.

Maud rushed to Montreal to be with her best friend. Her presence seemed to have a magical effect. As soon as Frede laid eyes on Maud, she began to recover. Miraculously, and against the doctors' predictions, Frede survived the typhoid fever.

That summer, Maud returned to Prince Edward Island for a visit, but for the first time, she was reluctant to leave Leaskdale. She suffered from morning sickness, and she kept one eye always on the war news. More than that, she had a premonition that this visit home would not be happy or easy. Indeed, she was met almost at once with news that the mother of one of her childhood friends had died. She had dreamed one of her eerie dreams about that friend just a few months earlier.

One night, Maud slipped out of the Cavendish manse and walked over the church grounds, along the meadow's edge, past the spruce grove till her grandparents' house "lay before me in a soft, silvery shadow." She stood beneath the window of her old room. It seemed Grandmother was alive and waiting; that the cat Daffy played nearby, her school friends surrounded her, and her own white bed lay waiting for her to return. It was a strange, enchanted stay among the ruins of the old house—and for a half an hour, the lost world breathed for her again.

Yet when Maud returned to Leasksdale with Frede at her side, she declared her homecoming one of the rare "perfect" moments of her life. Children, gardens, cats— all her loved ones dazzled her. She also arrived home to find the first copy of *Anne of the Island* waiting between brand-new covers.

That book marked a close in Anne's chapters in several ways. Maud was certain that she was at last done with writing about Anne. And *Anne of the Island* marked the end— at last!—of her long five-year contract with L. C. Page & Company. They had rejected a volume of her war poems; another company seemed interested. Perhaps at last, her publishing career could take a new turn.

On October 7, 1915, ten days earlier than expected, Maud gave birth to a healthy ten-pound baby boy. They named him Ewan Stuart Macdonald, but always called him Stuart. Half an hour after his birth, he lifted his head and looked around him "with bright wide-open eyes." That quality of alert intelligence would prove true all his life; Stuart was the easygoing darling of the family. He could never replace the baby who had died, but Stuart gave Maud another reason to overcome the sadness and anxiety of those years.

Meanwhile, the war in Europe edged closer to home. Maud's youngest half brother, Carl, her father's son from his second marriage, was injured on the battlefield and left to lie in the bitter cold for eighteen hours. As a result, he lost one leg. He resembled Hugh John both in looks and in his gentle warmth of personality, and Maud loved him dearly. She called Carl his "father's son and my full brother."

The following year brought a string of illnesses to the house. Stuart did not grow as quickly as he should. Chester, always a healthy, easy baby, began to suffer from one illness after another. He slept poorly and suffered from stomach upsets. Maud was a fretful mother. She worried especially about her "dear little Chester, the core of my heart since his birth — my first born." Maud came down with the grippe, and Ewan fell ill with a protracted case of bronchitis and laryngitis. As usual, Maud pasted a smile over her worries, "a mask and . . . a cheerfulness I am far from feeling."

As president of the Red Cross, Maud forced herself

out of her sickbed and ran a "pie social." In the old days, she had won the highest bids from the handsomest young men in town, whose reward would be to eat the pie in her company. Now the bid went to "an awkward schoolboy who could say nothing and to whom I could say nothing." They ate the pie in silence, and Maud felt "as if every mouthful must choke me."

She had discovered gray hairs threaded among the brown. Maud had always admired silver hair—in others. But now her age seemed another sign of loss. Maud's earnings had dropped off from their peak of a few years earlier. Ewan's salary had always been small. The family depended heavily on Maud's income, and with two growing boys and a husband whose ambitions seemed doomed to fail at every turn, she could not afford to slow down for an instant.

Ewan's funds toward a foreign mission had fallen far short of the goal. Maud remained his chief benefactor. She had predicted, rightly, that Ontario farmers would be unmoved by appeals to send money to far-flung places. Ewan's career stalled. He was not offered a new ministry in Toronto or anywhere else.

People who knew Ewan at this time described him as secretive and hard to read. As had happened in Scotland, Ewan considered his failures a sign that he was cursed by God. This line of thought would lay him low time and again. He helped to found a wartime committee dedicated to helping bereaved families, but Ewan's own spirits were often troubled, and he became more and more silent and withdrawn, both at home and at church.

Maud's world revolved around her children, her work, and the war. She posted a map of Europe in the manse. She kept up with three newspapers each day. In November 1916, her first book of war poems, *The Watchman and Other Poems,* appeared. Almost the only relief that year came when Frede arrived for a precious Christmas visit, and then the house rang with unaccustomed laughter.

In 1916, Maud returned again to her character Anne—but with a new publisher. In Toronto, Maud had met with the editor of McClelland, Goodchild & Stewart, a Canadian publishing company. Not only did McClelland publish *The Watchman,* but Maud promised them her next novel, *Anne's House of Dreams.* This was her darkest fiction yet, about the friendship between Anne and her mysterious neighbor, Leslie Moore. Leslie is trapped in a loveless marriage to a man paralyzed with physical and mental problems. In the end, she learns she has been married to a stranger masquerading as her fiancé—and is finally set free. The plot doubtless reflected some of Maud's musings about her own troubled marriage. Ewan was not the man he had seemed either—but Maud would find no easy way out.

Writing, for Maud, was an act of preservation. "The world can never be the same again," she confided in her journal. "Our old world has passed away forever." Yet that vanished world is kept alive in *Anne's House of Dreams,* a book that explores the meaning of friendship, rescue, and finding home. The story is deeply rooted in Prince Edward Island, and celebrates the joy of belonging to a close-knit community—even while Maud was mourning its loss.

Maud began at this time a short memoir, written in a sequence of articles for a popular women's magazine. These articles were later collected and published as a book, *The Alpine Path.* The memoir focused almost solely on Maud's writing life. She managed to evade writing about her marriage, focusing instead on childhood, ancestry, Prince Edward Island, and literature. Though she had loved Herman Leard passionately, "I was never in love with Ewan—never have been in love with him," she confided to her journal. She was "fond" of her husband, and grateful for having been rescued from a lonely life. None of those facts, she declared, had any place in her memoir.

The years 1918 and 1919 were arguably two of the worst in Maud's life. She claimed that after 1919, she was never entirely happy again. The yeard 1918 began terrifyingly. One night in January, Maud felt a hard lump in her breast. She was sure she was dying of cancer. Maud did not feel she could consult the local doctor, for fear of his gossipy wife spreading the news. Instead she visited a doctor in Montreal who, after a series of tests, assured her that the lump was benign.

Maud barely had time to feel her relief when the latest terrifying war news eclipsed personal concerns. Ewan came through the door, asking, "Do you want to hear the latest news from the front?" A friend had written to say that the British line had broken, and Germans were raining gun shells down on Paris. Maud nearly collapsed. If Paris was lost, all was lost. It was days till Maud learned the true facts. Meanwhile she paced the parlor floor, wringing her hands and murmuring, "Oh God, oh God."

Maud turned to Veronal tablets to help her sleep. Veronal was a sleeping pill, a hypnotic and barbiturate that was addictive and potentially deadly. There was many a "hellish week of up and downs" on the war front when Maud stopped eating, barely slept, and depended heavily on these pills.

Even her visit to Prince Edward Island that summer failed to rouse her. Maud missed her daily newspapers and felt out of touch with the world. Change was afoot on her beloved island. The beautiful woods behind her schoolhouse had been chopped down. Cars with their noise and dust had come at last to Prince Edward Island — the last Canadian province to lift the ban. In Cavendish, Maud found one of her old schoolmates, Lizzie Stewart Laird, in a terrible state. Lizzie had spent a year in an insane asylum and more years struggling against mental illness. The two old friends exchanged kindly words, but Maud came away heartsore. The Lizzie she'd known as a child didn't exist anymore.

During that same visit, Maud returned again to the old Macneill homestead. But there was no enchanting moonlight to soften the scene this time—instead she found only "the woeful desolation of everything." Uncle John had let the homestead decay and collapse. The front door was held closed by a single wire.

Maud did what she had never expected to do again in this life—she walked inside her grandparents' house. She stood in the kitchen and imagined herself back into the past. Ignoring the odor of decay, she made her way into the parlor and dining room, and began to mount the stairs to her old room, that "illimitable kingdom" of her youth. But she stopped at the threshold. Her precious room was too full of "ghosts—lonely, hungry ghosts." Such visits were too eerie, the sweetness too mixed with the bitter. "I will make no more of them," she swore.

Shadows were approaching, and nothing would ward them off. That July, Maud helped host a large dinner party at Park Corner. It was a jovial gathering, including Frede's brother, George; his wife, Ella, and their little son, Georgie; Aunt Annie; Maud, Stuart, and Chester; and others. Maud took a head count and came up with thirteen.

Jokingly she pointed out the unlucky number—then immediately regretted it, for Ella was pregnant, unhappy, and feeling ill. To cover her mistake, Maud smilingly said, "Frede, you were the thirteenth to sit down—the omen must be for you."

Frede at once jumped up from the table and refused to take her seat again. It didn't matter how much the others teased or begged her to come back. Frede ate her dinner on the porch. That night, Maud and Frede stayed up late, chatting and confiding, and all of their immediate worries—including the unlucky thirteen at the table— were forgotten. Yet when Maud left the Campbells' a week later, she sobbed uncontrollably, "as if I never expected to see Park Corner again."

Instead, Park Corner came to see Maud—in the form of Aunt Annie. Maud was delighted to have her company, made still sweeter on October 6, 1918, by the news that Germany and Austria had at last surrendered, marking an end to the terrible war. The date, Maud declared, "should be written in capitals—in letters of gold." Maud was so thrilled, she called every friend in town and ran outside to put up the flag. "Sit down, child," said Aunt Annie calmly.

As fall turned to winter, Maud fell ill with the Spanish flu. She came close to pneumonia and was bedridden for days. While she lay ill, a letter came from Aunt Annie telling that her only son, George, one of the thirteen diners at that unlucky table, had died. Soon followed a heartbreaking letter adding that little Georgie, George and Ella's young son, had succumbed to the deadly flu as well.

Ella and Aunt Annie were sick from shock; the other children ill with the flu. Frede hurried home to manage things as best she could. Once again, Maud flew to her cousin's rescue. When she arrived, everyone was sick in bed except Frede. They stayed up all night talking, "rinsing out their souls."

Park Corner had fallen on hard times emotionally and financially. The two cousins, Maud and Frede, put their heads together to discuss things as calmly as they could. They cleaned and disinfected the house. They placed their hope for Park Corner's future on one of the younger Campbells, Dan, "a fine smart lad, industrious and thrifty . . . a new streak in the Campbells." Maud had loaned money to her late cousin George and vowed not to take a penny's interest on the loan. Somehow, Maud and Frede promised each other, they would manage to pull through.

On the evening of Armistice Day, November 11, 1918, Frede and Maud strolled together in the dark and walked the lane across the Lake of Shining Waters. Now that the war was over, Frede was soon to be reunited with her soldier husband, Cam Macfarlane. Frede's engagement and marriage that spring had happened within six hours — so suddenly that it had left Maud feeling "dumbfounded, flabbergasted, knocked out and rendered speechless." She had not yet met Frede's husband—indeed, one might argue that Frede barely knew him herself.

Maud feared that her best friend had married in haste and would repent at leisure. Ever since the typhoid fever, Frede's heart had not been strong. "Oh Freddie-girl, I want you to be happy!" Maud wrote in her journal that day. "You have had so little happiness in your uneasy life."

At the year's end, despite all the recent sorrows, Maud finished her ninth novel, *Rainbow Valley*—an effervescent, dreamy book about Anne's children and their group of young friends. It was, as Robert Frost once wrote of great poetry, "a momentary stay against confusion."

But darkness loomed just ahead. Two of the thirteen at the unlucky table in Park Corner had already died of the flu. As 1918 turned the corner into the new year, Maud learned that her beloved Frede was desperately ill again in Montreal, this time with pneumonia. Maud had come to her cousin's rescue four years earlier; she believed she could perform a second miracle.

Maud arrived exhausted in Montreal on a Thursday night. Almost as soon as she laid eyes on Frede, white and still in her hospital bed, Maud knew there was no hope this time.

By dawn on Saturday, January 25, the doctors admitted they could do no more. Frede was kept calm on morphine. She lay muttering quietly to herself, her breathing hoarse and labored. Maud told Frede that she was going to write to Aunt Annie and wondered if Frede had any word to send her mother. "Yes. Tell her I want to know exactly how her hand is," she said. Frede's message to her new husband, Cam, was less "commonplace." She wished for him "the courage of the strong."

Maud summoned all her bravery for one last question. She didn't want to frighten Frede. But the cousins had agreed years earlier that whichever of them died first would visit the other and reassure them after death. Earnestly, Maud begged Frede not to forget her promise.

"You'll be sure to come, won't you?" Maud pleaded.

"Certainly," Frede said, loudly and distinctly. It was the last thing she said. She died just after dawn, quietly, "as a tired child might fall asleep."

Frede was the one great, enduring, irreplaceable love of Maud's life. Frede herself once told Maud, "there's nobody true—except you. You are the only person I've ever found whom I could trust absolutely." Maud adored her young cousin. She admired Frede; loved her intelligence and strength; depended on her good sense, her good humor, her laughter and wit. No one could raise Maud's spirits like Frede. No one else ever drew so close.

How, Maud thought frantically, how could she survive a life without Frede? Maud pictured the years stretching out empty before her, scene after scene of desolation. Not for the first time, Maud's imagination worked against her. All the pain and sadness that should have come upon her over time, "all the loneliness—all the longing—was concentrated in those hours." It marked a time "of horror" for Maud, who never completely reconciled herself to the loss.

The war had ended at last, but Maud could not be comforted over the death of Frede. Where, Maud asked in anguish, "is that unfailing humor, that flashing wit, that tender strength, that magnetic personality?" No answer could console her. "In all our great crises of life we have been together," wrote Maud. In this, her greatest crisis yet, Maud stood alone.

Later that spring, Ewan suffered his first complete nervous breakdown. He may have been responding to his wife's depression and despair. He may have finally realized, with the death of Frede, that he and Maud remained fundamentally separate. Perhaps he had been spiraling downward for a long time, unnoticed, unattended, and unable to rise.

Ewan hid his breakdown as best he could from his two congregations. Any form of mental illness was considered a shameful secret. Maud carefully hid the truth of her husband's psychological condition. She went to great lengths to preserve the myth that Ewan was only physically sick or exhausted. Sometimes she wrote his sermons for him, and poor Ewan stumbled through them as best he could.

But that May of the deadly year 1919—"the most terrible year of my life," Maud wrote—Ewan's condition was too desperate to hide, or to keep out of plain sight.

The crisis also marked a return of Ewan's religious demons. He became convinced that not only he but also Maud and their children were condemned to eternal damnation. Maud knew that when Ewan was in his right mind, he did not believe in an old-fashioned fire-and-brimstone hell any more than she did. But she recognized that this might be the symptom of true mental illness, and she was terrified that his sanity might never return.

That May, the Macdonalds were to host a number of high-powered, influential visiting ministers for several days. Initially, Ewan seemed fine, even jovial, though suffering from headaches and insomnia. Then suddenly, in the middle of the visit, he took to walking aimlessly in fields and lanes late at night. He fell into a silent, depressed lethargy. He would have nothing to do with the visiting ministers. All he could do was lie in his hammock, brooding over his own and the children's eternal damnation.

Maud took over all of the social obligations, staying up late with their visiting guests. She tried to explain away Ewan's behavior as the result of physical problems. When her newly married cousin Stella came for an ill-timed visit, Maud hid the problem from Stella as well. She begged Ewan to give up his late-night wanderings. But his condition continued to deteriorate. Finally, as a desperate measure, Maud sent him to his sister's in Boston.

There, doctors confirmed Maud's worst fears. They believed Ewan suffered from chronic "manic-depressive insanity." Maud's horror indicates that somehow she had still failed to connect this disorder with her own recurring severe mood swings. She began to plan for a future without him — she must get the children someplace safe, and find a good sanitarium for her husband.

The doctors did suggest one other possibility: Ewan might be suffering from kidney disease. Maud seized on this as something she could talk about to others. Ewan was told to drink plenty of water and given chloral tablets to help him sleep. Chloral hydrate, now illegal in the United States, was then used as a sedative and sleeping aid — sometimes even as an anesthetic. Its side effects on the heart and renal system could be deadly. Worse, Maud combined Ewan's dose of chloral with the sedative Veronal, thinking it would help Ewan sleep. Instead, he muttered and twitched restlessly all night, tapping and talking endlessly, like some monstrous version of her old fiancé, Edwin Simpson. Maud dared not leave her husband's side. While Ewan slept three or four hours a night, Maud lay awake.

Ewan's condition deteriorated all summer and into fall. No wonder Maud called 1919 "a hellish year." By September, Ewan slipped in and out of complete mental collaspe. Only now did Maud learn that this was not

Ewan's first brush with madness—he had suffered from religious melancholia both times he went away to college in Canada, and during his catastrophic trip to Glasgow.

Nothing roused or comforted him. He could barely be distracted for an instant from his brooding. He showed no interest in either of his sons. In fact, they only increased his sense of horror. Ewan told Maud he wished the children had never been born.

In these terrible, lonely days, Maud thought repeatedly of Frede's final promise, to reveal herself to Maud after death. So far, there had been no such visitation. One bleak afternoon, Maud sat with her cat Daffy and thought, "if you are here, make Daff come over to me and kiss me." Daffy was Maud's least affectionate pet. Immediately Daffy walked slowly across the room, placed his paw gently on her shoulder, and touched his mouth to Maud's cheek—not once, but twice. Maud clung to this reassurance as a sign.

Writing, for Maud, was rescue, escape, salvation, and purpose. She finished her tenth novel, *Rilla of Ingleside,* a book about World War I that she dedicated to Frede. Maud felt little enthusiasm for *Rilla,* which critics generally agree is one of Montgomery's weakest Anne books, uncharacteristically dark and sentimental. But its author was pleased at least when she sat down in 1919 and tallied her literary earnings. Maud had come a long way from her first five-dollar check from *Golden Days.* She had earned

257

close to $75,000 from her writing—a fortune in those days. With wry modesty, she described it as "not a bad showing, considering my initial equipment—my pen and scanty education."

Her youngest son, Stuart, too, was a comfort, always merry, affectionate, and bright, while his older brother Chester, at seven, had become a worry. Chester rarely showed open affection to anyone. Chester, like his father, was reserved and secretive. He took after his father in other ways, seeming almost entirely indifferent to nature's beauty, as was Ewan, whom Maud once described as being as "unaware of it as a blind man."

Stuart had an open, fervent nature, and was dedicated to Maud. He was a handsome, fair-haired boy with large, brilliant blue eyes and a rosy complexion. Stuart would tell his brother, "*You* have a father. This is my mother." The family divisions, later so deep and so painful, began to form even this early on.

Ewan had been stumbling along, barely getting through his days, when his longtime good friend the popular and energetic Reverend Edwin Smith came to Leaskdale for a visit. Edwin Smith was to Ewan what Frede had been to Maude. He was a confidant, trusted friend, and clerical brother. All the while that Maud kept sending Ewan to doctors, Ewan had been saying, "I need a minister." He may have been right. As Maud described it, "when he left to meet Captain Smith at the station he was very miserable. Two hours later, when he returned, he was well." Whatever Mr. Smith had said or done, it had a miraculous effect on Ewan.

Edwin Smith was everything Ewan was not: successful, vivacious, charismatic, boyishly handsome. Even into his fifties, Smith looked no more than thirty-five. In photographs of the best friends standing side by side, Edwin, the elder minister, looks young enough to be Ewan's son. Smith was also a war hero. The first time Maud ever laid eyes on him, a friend commented, "That man is too good-looking to be a minister."

Edwin Smith brought out the best in Maud, too. He became, in his own masculine way, the kind of figure that Frede had been—magnetic, brilliant, full of life. Maud relished his visits and called Smith a "universal genius." At the heart of Maud and Ewan's marriage was a great void. Edwin Smith helped fill that emptiness. Maud never forgot the miracle he accomplished that September of 1919.

With Ewan on the mend, Maud could at last turn her attention elsewhere. Trouble was brewing on the publishing front. Now that the Great War was over, she found herself embroiled in a private war with her old publisher, L. C. Page & Company. Her adversary was wealthy and ruthless. She needed all her resources, stubbornness, and courage for the battles ahead.

CHAPTER NINETEEN

A Woman "They Cannot Bluff, Bully, or Cajole"

In 1918, Maud had received an unexpected Christmas present. It was an expensive travel book, inscribed to her by her old publisher, Louis C. Page: "Merry Christmas and Happy New Year. L. C. P." The gift was all the more surprising because Maud was in the midst of a lawsuit against the Page publishing company—a legal struggle that, as it turned out, would drag on for more than a decade.

Maud had earlier brought suit against a poet who had plagiarized her work in a magazine. Maud had also sued the Page company over a missing chapter from *Kilmeny of the Orchard*. She had won both of these cases, and now she steeled herself to go to court again.

This took grit. The Page Company—and Louis Page, in particular—was a formidable foe. Many authors, especially women authors, simply backed down in the face of his ferocious opposition. Page was a force to contend with, personally and financially, and Maud admitted that she was afraid of him. Louis Page was used to controlling his female authors, by turns courting, soothing, and threatening them. But as Maud wrote, she was one woman the Page Company would discover "they cannot bluff, bully, or cajole."

Louis Page was a graduate of Harvard University. Early on, Maud described him as "one of the most fascinating men I have ever met." He seems to have been the magnetic type, to whom she was most susceptible. Louis Page had green eyes and long, dark lashes that he used to good effect. Maud was initially taken by his "distinguished appearance and charming manner," and she also recorded in her journal that he came from a "fine old family." The young author was dazzled by her publisher's credentials. Yet she had also written, "The fact is that I do not trust him." As it turned out, her instincts were wise.

The terms of Maud's first contracts with Page were poor even by the day's standards. She received only a 10 percent royalty instead of the usual 15 percent, and that was based on the wholesale price of the book instead of the full retail price. Again and again, Maud failed to raise her royalty rate. But in 1915 she managed to omit the clause that guaranteed Page the right to all of her future books—freeing herself from them, or so she believed. With the publication of *Anne of the Island,* Maud's contract with Page expired. But Maud foresaw trouble ahead and joined the newly formed Authors League of America as an extra precaution.

Meanwhile, she had sold the rights to her next book— *The Watchman and Other Poems*—to the Canadian firm of McClelland, Goodchild & Stewart. McClelland also agreed to act as Maud's literary agent in the United States. The Page Company angrily threatened suit over these arrangements, even though they themselves had turned down the book of poems.

There was some talk of the Page Company working together with McClelland. But the Pages proved impossible to deal with. First, Louis Page declared that he would have nothing to do with McClelland. Then he wrote to McClelland on the sly to reopen negotiations. But Page was too late. Maud had already signed a contract with the American publisher Frederick A. Stokes Company. Their terms were generous. The Stokes Company agreed to pay Maud 20 percent royalties and a $5,000 advance.

When the Page Company caught wind of this, they withheld $1,000 from Maud's next royalty check, claiming they had made a mistake in an earlier royalty report. They also began selling reprint rights without her permission. If McClelland had become Maud's agent in America, then

Page would become her reprint agent—whether she liked it or not.

Maud did not like it. She also knew that Page was withholding the $1,000 unfairly. In January 1919, just days before Frede's final illness, Maud traveled to Boston to prepare for her first day in court. She was surprised how much Louis Page had aged—he looked dissipated and old; his way of life, she declared, had finally caught up with him. But she found it hard to pity the man who had run her around in circles for so long. In 1917, she had confided to her journal, "If Page is not honourable I am no match for him." Now, two years later, she was determined to prove herself wrong.

Maud was a good witness. While Louis Page kept licking his lips and playing with his watch, Maud remained calm and collected. In private, she would go up to her hotel room and cry after the hours in court—but no one would have known it from her coolness on the stand. Nor would they know that she always left feeling she had "made an incredible ass of myself." The clear, eloquent voice recorded in the transcripts surprised Maud each time she heard it. Even the opposing lawyer complimented her on her composure, though, she noted wryly, that wouldn't prevent him from "grilling me in his best style in the witness box."

The Page Company was anxious enough to offer Maud a settlement. They proposed $10,000, but Maud demanded $18,000. Page countered with $17,000. Maud held firm. She won her $18,000, but in the midst of her celebration came the devastating news about Frede. Maud left directly from Boston to Montreal. For a time, Frede's death pushed every other thought aside.

Maud's settlement proved less victorious than it first appeared. She settled with Page for $17,880 for *all* of the rights to her first seven works. What she didn't know was that Page already was in the midst of negotiating film rights to *Anne of Green Gables*—for $40,000.

Had Maud held out a little longer, she would have earned $20,000 on that first movie deal alone. As it turned out, she never saw a penny of that money, or indeed of *any* film or dramatic rights to *Anne of Green Gables*.

The first Hollywood film version of *Anne,* a silent movie, was released that same year. Maud resented the loss of income, she thought the film badly cast, and last but not least, Hollywood had added some offensive Americanisms. They added scenes that never appeared in the book, including one adventure featuring a skunk— an animal unknown to Prince Edward Island. In another scene, Maud spotted an American flag flying over Anne's schoolhouse. "Crass, blatant Yankeeism!" she fumed.

If the Page brothers, Louis and George, had under-estimated Maud, she had underestimated them as well. Back in 1912, Maud had submitted stories to the Pages for her book *Chronicles of Avonlea*. The Pages chose the stories they liked best and threw out the rest—or so Maud had believed. Now it turned out that they had made copies of all the rejected stories, kept them, and were planning to publish them without her permission as *Further Chronicles of Avonlea.*

Maud had already used selections of those rejected stories in other works. If they reappeared now, it would look as if she had run out of material and was recycling old work. Worse, many of these old stories were about Anne Shirley. Her new contract with the American publisher specified that she couldn't print anything new about Anne with any other company.

The Pages chose a red-haired heroine for the cover of *Further Chronicles of Avonlea,* taking advantage of the popularity of red-haired Anne Shirley. In court, lawyers and witnesses spent hours debating the exact shade of red in that cover girl's hair, trying to decide if it suggested Anne. Was it carroty? Or a shade more auburn?

This first suit was followed by more suits and countersuits. The Pages filed a suit against Maud for "malicious litigation." Next they sued for libel, first in the Massachusetts Supreme Court, and then, when that was struck down, in the United States Supreme Court. The legal expenses on both sides were horrendous—and so was the cost to Maud's nerves. One summer, Maud spent more than a month away from home dealing with the lawsuits—missing even Chester's birthday.

By 1919, Maud was sick to death of writing about Anne. In 1921 she published the last chronological book in the Anne series, *Rilla of Ingleside,* about Anne's nearly grown-up daughter. Finally, she declared, she was "done with Anne forever." She wrote to her old friend George MacMillan, "I swear it as a dark and deadly vow." Maud had long wished to create a "new heroine," a feat she accomplished brilliantly with the character of Emily Starr, the aspiring young writer at the center of *Emily of New Moon.*

Emily Starr resembles her creator, L. M. Montgomery—and her earlier creation, Anne—in many ways. Like Maud, Emily lives with elderly relatives; she uses letterbills on which to scribble her stories; she is imaginative, beauty loving, and outspoken. But Emily has a sharper edge than did Anne Shirley; she is thornier and less innocent. Readers embraced *Emily of New Moon,* and critics praised it as Maud's best work since *Anne of Green Gables. Emily* was dedicated to Maud's ever-loyal pen pal, Scotsman George MacMillan, "in recognition of a long and stimulating friendship."

It was not till late 1928 that the last of the suits between Maud and Page was resolved. Over that long, litigious decade, Maud managed somehow to keep her head above water. She had made it clear that she was a force to be reckoned with. And through the legal and emotional storms, she kept right on writing and publishing. She published two more Emily books: *Emily Climbs* and *Emily's Quest,* although, as ever, she felt her sequels were weaker than the original. She wished she had the leisure to write her books more slowly and thoughtfully. Still, as Maud confided to MacMillan, "I can't afford to damn the public. I must cater to it for awhile."

The Page Company had cost Maud—and themselves—thousands of dollars in legal expenses, each side believing that they could hold out longest. In the end, Maud triumphed. Public opinion turned slowly but surely against Louis Page and his unfair business dealings. When the renowned Wanamaker's department store stopped carrying Page's books, Louis Page had finally reached his limit. Maud had predicted this would happen, though she never dreamed that the court fights would be so ferocious or last so long. "I shall win because I can afford to lose and the Pages can't," she had written in her journal.

She prevailed where other writers would have long ago surrendered. The famous Macneill stubbornness held her in good stead all during those fighting years.

Ewan, meanwhile, continued his own more private, personal battle with mental illness. He fought against chronic depression and recurring bouts of paralyzing religious terrors. He mixed sleeping pills with bromides, and his already poor memory began to desert him. Sometimes he simply could not perform his duties. He slept from eight at night till noon the next day. Maud covered for him as best she could.

Chester, the firstborn, much-loved darling, had developed into a problem child. He got into chronic trouble at school, with friends, with the domestic help, and especially with girls. Maud made excuses for him, blaming his troubles on the people around him, but even she began to have her doubts.

There was disappointment for her on the literary front as well. A new, more "serious" cosmopolitan and realistic fiction was now in vogue. The most influential critics in Canada dismissed Maud's books. William Arthur Deacon attacked her "series of girls' sugary stories." Maud was left out of public events and ousted from committees. She felt less welcome in Toronto's literary society.

But there were still rewards and delights to uphold Maud in these years. Stuart, her younger son, succeeded in everything he tried — academics, athletics, friendship. Stuart's sweet-tempered company compensated for the lack of companionship she felt with her elder son, Chester, or her husband, Ewan.

In 1923, Maud became the first Canadian woman admitted to the British Royal Society of the Arts. She accumulated thousands of loyal fans with each new book. Maud was invited to meet the Prince of Wales and received a fan letter from British prime minister Stanley Baldwin himself, addressed to her from the famous 10 Downing Street.

Even when she had a house full of company, part of Maud's mind was always occupied with whatever she was writing. Visitors witnessed these mysterious internal dialogues. Sometimes she would stand stock-still, laugh aloud as if in surprise, and murmur, "Why, that's what I'll do! That's *exactly* what I'll do"—and rush off to jot down a note or scene. She kept a notebook and pen in her apron pocket for these small literary "emergencies."

In 1922, Maud also fell in love again, perhaps for the last time—and with a place, not a person. The family took a trip to Muskoka, the beautiful lake district ninety miles north of Toronto. It was a popular, lively vacation spot in summer. At night the town of Bala was illuminated by colored lanterns, and dances were held at the large dance pavilion. Maud found it "more like fairyland than any place I ever saw"—with dozens of tiny islands, lakes, a river, an open bay, deep woods, and handsome summer cottages.

John Mustard—Maud's once-upon-a-time nemesis, teacher, and suitor—had built a summer cottage just north of Bala with his sons. Mustard was as youthful, fit, handsome, and capable as Ewan Macdonald was now stodgy, slow, and clumsy. The contrast between the two men must have been painful—but Maud responded as she had all her life, by retreating into her imagination.

That summer she had some of the "sweet-lipped soli-tude" she craved, when John Mustard kindly took Ewan and the boys out on his boat, or back at their own board-inghouse while Ewan accompanied the boys on outings by the lake. Maud spent one such evening intensely day-dreaming on the veranda.

She wrote to George MacMillan how she had "dreamed it all out to the end of September." In her mind she peopled Lake Muskoka with all of her beloveds, the living and the dead. Frede was there, of course, and Aunt Annie, Bertie McIntyre, Ewan and the boys (in her daydream, "Ewan was not a minister!"), and George MacMillan, too, was there. Maud had always possessed a preternatural ability to remove herself from a real situa-tion into a dreamscape more vivid.

Now, on the veranda of a boardinghouse, she dreamed her way into a lakeside Eden. She cooked and served imag-inary meals. In her fantasy, George MacMillan, Ewan, and the boys were caught in a storm on the lake, while she and Frede held a lantern by the shore and awaited the men's safe return. It may have been "silly and babyish," or even "crazy," she admitted, but Maud's vivid dream life was like a second existence. And it often provided rich material for her writing.

In 1926, Maud made one other debut—she published her first novel for adults, *The Blue Castle*. It was set not on Prince Edward Island but in the Muskoka Lake district.

The Blue Castle is a wry, tender, unorthodox romance, one of Montgomery's most fully realized works. It is a testament to her happy summer at Muskoka, and to her undimmed capacity for dreaming. It also served as an apology to another one-time nemesis, the motorcar. Cars had "nothing romantic about them," Maud once declared, grateful that she had been courted in the era of the horse and buggy. But she came to see the romantic potential in speed and escape—and to learn firsthand about the danger of these newfangled machines.

CHAPTER TWENTY

Dashing over the Traces

In 1918, Prince Edward Island became the last province in Canada to legalize the motorcar, and Maud's sympathy lay with the stubborn islanders. She loved skimming along snowy and moonlit roads behind a horse and buggy. Maud's most important courting had happened on carriage rides—those precious stolen moments when Herman Leard had nestled her head on his shoulder, and the evening Ewan proposed.

But Maud also relished movement and change. When she made a list of everything she liked best in 1920, she included "motoring and driving," noting that she enjoyed "a systematic life with occasional dashings over the traces."

She and Ewan bought their first motorcar in 1918—a five-passenger Chevrolet. Only a few years earlier, cars were unheard-of in Leaskdale, and the mere sound of one was enough to set the whole neighborhood running. By 1918, automobiles had become commonplace. Maud earned more than $45,000 in royalties that year.

Maud was never brave enough to drive herself, and was by all accounts a nervous passenger. One family friend remembered Maud clutching frantically at the insides of the car. Maud described herself as a backseat driver. "I content myself with poking Mr. Mac. in the back with my parasol if I think he is going more than 20 miles, and saying, 'Beware' in a sepulchral tone when I see him preparing to turn a corner."

Ewan was a remarkably poor and clumsy driver. According to biographer Mary Rubio, "Ewan was maladroit when it came to anything practical or mechanical." He had trouble remembering that he was not still driving a horse and buggy, and when he needed to stop the car quickly, he was likely to pull back on the steering wheel and holler "Whoa! Whoa!"

Early automobiles started by hand with a crank. Ewan had a hard time managing the trick. The Macdonalds regularly burst a tire on the rough road to Zephyr, and it was not uncommon for an axle to fall off. By 1921, Ewan had already gotten into a series of fender benders, and Maud decided that their Chevrolet was not sturdy enough to withstand all the wear and tear. So they bought a new, elegant Canadian Gray-Dort touring car the family nick-named Lady Jane Grey.

Unfortunately, Lady Jane Grey provided no guarantee against mishaps. A month after they'd purchased the new car, Ewan came to a blind corner of a crossroads and crashed into an oncoming speeding Chevrolet. Both cars sustained damage, though no one appeared badly hurt. Lady Jane Grey had a bent axle, a crushed fender, and a broken headlamp. The Chevrolet reported eighty-five dollars in damages.

The Macdonalds were unlucky. The man driving the Chevrolet was the cranky, warlike Marshall Pickering, an elder in the Zephyr Methodist church. Maud thought her own husband to blame for his careless driving but Pickering equally to blame for speeding. The Pickerings insisted *all* the fault lay with Ewan. The next day, Marshall Pickering went to the hospital due to a "stoppage of urine." (Pickering had suffered from prostate troubles for many years, and had been treated for this same medical problem previously.)

Ewan called on Mrs. Pickering to express his sympathy for her husband. She made snappish remarks about Ewan's poor driving. The minister then visited Marshall Pickering in the hospital. There he met Pickering's son, who confided that his father had arranged for a prostate operation a month earlier.

All Zephyr was buzzing with news of the accident. If automobiles were rare, automobile accidents were even rarer. For a while, the two-car pileup was all that the folks in Zephyr could talk about.

In December of 1921 Maud had another one of her strange, predictive dreams. In it, she came home to find that Ewan was hanged and had come back to life. As if in answer to the dream, the Pickerings presented a bizarre Christmas gift to the Macdonalds: a letter demanding $500 toward Marshall Pickering's prostate operation.

Needless to say, the Macdonalds were flabbergasted— Maud outraged, Ewan distressed. The letter's angry and demanding tone bothered them both. Had they been asked to pay for car repairs, they would have considered making amends, but to pay for a man's already-scheduled prostate surgery was out of the question. Ewan earned only $1,500 a year for ministering to both his churches. But Maud was a wealthy woman, as the Pickerings knew.

Ewan wrote back, explaining that since both parties had been at fault, both should pay equally for the damages. He also noted that Pickering's prostate troubles had begun long before the accident.

Pickering responded—by raising his demand to $1,500! When Ewan fought back—canvassing neighbors, hiring his own lawyer—Pickering raised the stakes yet again, now suing for $8,000: $1,000 for his operation,

$5,000 for his sufferings, and another $2,000 for his wife. Pickering was a powerful but unpopular man. One neighbor exclaimed, "Eight thousand!! It's more than his whole damned carcass is worth."

In the end, the local judge for the case inexplicably decided for Pickering, awarding him $1,000 for his operation, $500 for sufferings, and more than $1,000 for his wife. Granted, Pickering had connections in high places. But witnesses from the community declared themselves flabbergasted.

This wasn't the only unpleasant battle raging around the Macdonalds. The idea of church union was in the air. It began with the Anglicans, who proposed a United Church of Canada. Over the next few decades, the idea of a single Canadian United Church gained more support, and by the early 1920s, church union, as it was known, seemed likely to take place.

Ewan stood to lose more than he gained by union. He was no longer an especially popular or effective minister; he had fallen a long way from the eager young man who set off in search of a brilliant career. Church union would mean a consolidation of ministries and a loss of jobs. What's more, a Methodist minister was already in place in Zephyr, and there was no guarantee that Ewan would be chosen over him. Nonetheless, Ewan told a friend that he was not entirely opposed to union, but that Maud was dead set against it. She feared the United Church would become a large, impersonal bureaucracy, "ruled by a few at the top." Ever the fierce loyalist, she clung to her Scottish Presbyterian ancestry.

In the end, the United Church of Canada was voted forward by a strong majority of Congregationalists, Methodists, and about two-thirds of Presbyterians. The remaining one-third of Presbyterians stayed separate as "Continuing Presbyterians." The Macdonalds were among this minority, and as Maud wrote to MacMillan, life was "made unhappy for us by the terrible . . . disruption in our church."

In Leaskdale, there was only the one Presbyterian church in town, and the local community supported Ewan as minister. But in Zephyr, things turned acrimonious. While Leaskdale voted solidly to remain Continuing Presbyterian, Zephyr's smaller community was more divided, voting only twenty-three to eighteen to stay Presbyterian.

The whole business left a bitter taste for the Macdonalds. Ewan, in particular, was relieved when in late 1925 he was chosen to lead a new church in nearby Norval. Norval was closer to Toronto, where Chester was attending a private high school.

Maud and Ewan had been taking turns falling in and out of serious depressions for years. Both hoped a change of place might do the family good. Ewan had felt briefly energized by his legal battle against Marshall Pickering, but fell into despondency when he lost the case. He was ready to move without regret. For Maud, the move from Leaskdale to Norval was wrenching. She had put down roots; there in Leaskdale she had raised her boys. When it came time to say good-bye, she was tearful even at parting from the difficult congregants in Zephyr. Ewan felt no such sorrow.

The Norval manse was a large, handsome brick house, with indoor plumbing and electricity. Once again, Ewan would serve two local churches—one at Norval, and one in Glen Williams—but the parishioners of both congregations were equally well-to-do and friendly. The town of Norval appealed to Maud at once, and reminded her of beloved Cavendish. It was friendly, green, and rural, with a river running through it, yet was close to a railway line that could bring her swiftly into Toronto. Maud bragged to George MacMillan, "It is one of the beauty spots of Ontario."

Maud fell in love especially with the hill of pines rising up behind the manse. She watched the bright moonlight beaming over those pines; it filled a longing as nothing had since she had left Prince Edward Island. The beauty-hungry girl in Maud never died. Here in Norval she found a natural beauty to nourish her.

The only bad news was that their new church treasurer was engaged to a relative of none other than Marshall

Pickering, their driving adversary from Zephyr. Ewan had evaded the court judgment because he had no money to pay—and the court could not force him to use Maud's money. But the very evening before they were to move to Norval, Ewan received warning that anything shipped by rail in his name would be seized on behalf of Marshall Pickering. The family quickly changed the labels on all the boxes to "Mrs. Macdonald."

Maud was initially energized by the move. She published both her adult novels—*The Blue Castle* and *The Tangled Web*—as well as a number of children's novels: *Emily's Quest, Magic for Marigold, Pat of Silver Bush,* and *Mistress Pat,* a sequel. She embarked on a reading tour of Western Canada, where at last she met her long-term pen pal Ephraim Weber and his wife. In Western Canada she also joyfully reunited with the now-married Laura Pritchard, sister of sweet "kindred spirit" Will Pritchard from Prince Albert days. Maud described the reunion: "We would embrace and kiss—draw back—look at each other—embrace again." It was proof, Maud affirmed, "that love was immortal."

Maud had long since stopped believing in a traditional Christian afterlife. Sometimes she maintained there was no God at all, only science and "blind impersonal Chance." Yet she believed in reincarnation, and in "an infinite ceaseless struggle" between good and evil. Of course, as she confessed to Ephraim Weber, she never discussed any of their unorthodox opinions in public. "I have to be exceedingly careful for my ministerial husband's sake."

Maud actively involved herself in the new Norval church. She still loved "making things go," as when helping out in the young people's theatrical events. She was less fond of the endless rounds of mission bands, auxiliaries, Women's Institutes, and Ladies' Aids. "Sometimes I get so sick of them that I could hang myself on the handiest gooseberry bush rather than go to another," she admitted.

Ewan continued to suffer from periodic depressions during these years, and his memory worsened. Maud wondered what his congregation would think if they could see him at home—pawing at his head; frantically intoning psalms against damnation; staring off into space with a half-frightened, half-vacant expression. Maud herself suffered from increasingly dark moods and anxieties about her sons—Chester especially, who seemed "girl crazy" when young, and something worse as he grew older. Chester exercised little control over his impulses. His social skills, never strong to begin with, degenerated over time.

Chester was bright but had a hard time settling in to anything, especially his studies. Like his father, he was overweight, clumsy, and unathletic. When Chester could not earn things honestly, he stole them—at first it was something as simple as a handful of cookies or attention; later on it would be money and valuables.

Both Ewan and Chester were strangely affectless. Their reactions struck many people as abnormal. Father and elder son were enough alike that they clashed with each other constantly.

Maud began worrying about Chester in a deep, sick-hearted way in 1928, but we do not know precisely what sent her into panic mode. Her journal entries are deliberately vague. There was an awful incident in which he exposed himself to one of their domestic household workers—but Maud kept this incident well under wraps. Whatever triggered Maud's anxiety was "something nasty and worrying that embittered life." For once, she could not confide even in her "grumble" journal, or in her trusty pen pals. Her habit of secretly obsessing about Chester would continue to the bitter end.

Stuart remained the stable, successful son. She began describing Stuart in her journals as her one "good son." She became fearful and clinging. Stuart and a friend left on their own one night to go ice-skating, and the ensuing hunt for both boys—though it ended happily—fractured Maud's already fragile nerves. Another time, Stuart nearly drowned when the Norval dam broke while he was swimming. After that, Maud was afraid to let him near the river that had twice almost claimed him.

When Stuart left for boarding school, Maud missed

him terribly. "This house is always strangely empty when Stuart's laugh has gone out of it." She could not turn to Ewan for strength, comfort, or even companionship. Over the years, husband and wife had drifted steadily further apart.

Ewan's resentment of Maud's fame and of her local popularity increased over time. When Maud's Sunday-school class presented her with a basket of Christmas roses, her husband turned away without a word. And though they all depended on the income from her work, Ewan was clearly not an L. M. Montgomery fan. Maud wrote in her journal, "Ewan secretly hates my work—and openly ignores it."

More and more, Maud came to rely on their hired help to get through her days. She depended on her household workers for the externals of her life, and she and Ewan both depended heavily on the few psychotropic drugs available. Unfortunately, the medicine that helped in one way harmed them in others. Ewan Macdonald was now taking a potentially deadly cocktail mix of tranquilizers, bromides, and sleeping pills. It made him sleepy, vague, and irritable, and it further eroded his failing memory. Maud, too, self-medicated with sleeping pills, wine, and tranquilizers. Starting in 1930, she began taking hypodermics, too, first for allergies, then for nerves.

There was no widespread acknowledgment of bipolar condition during Maud's lifetime; manic depressives were told to rest and were kept away from things that excited or stimulated them. Virginia Woolf, Maud's contemporary, was ordered to stop writing altogether. Luckily, Maud's husband did not often urge upon her that particular cure. Only as long as Maud was still able to write and escape into stories could she survive.

Some of the family's household helpers proved more helpful than others. Maud grew enormously fond of the lively Elsie Busby, for instance, but was horrified one night when she heard Elsie, her voice coming clearly through the heating grate, announcing that she "hated the Macdonalds." A few days later, the distraught author discovered that Elsie had combed through her private notes.

Maud lived in fear of that early childhood refrain "What will people say?" The idea that a maid knew her secrets and could easily spread them abroad appalled her. She fired Elsie immediately, but Elsie's successors were not all improvements. A maid named Margaret was, according to Mary Rubio, "eccentric and morose, with few skills in either housekeeping or cooking." Another worker gossiped incessantly. But a minister's wife could not afford to be a harsh or particular mistress. Sometimes Maud kept workers on simply because she was afraid to fire them.

The Great Depression, which financially devastated the lives of so many, also struck the Macdonald family. Some of the companies Maud had invested in heavily were failing. In 1930, one $14,000 investment's value fell to less than $2,000. Another $3,000 investment in a Toronto insurance company failed entirely. By the end of 1932, Maud was typing her own manuscripts for the first time in years, to avoid paying a professional typist. Though Maud was still wealthy by most standards, she had suffered serious losses and believed that her family stood near collapse. Would she have enough money to put both her boys through college? Maud had once believed they were well set for Ewan's retirement, but the 1929 stock market crash shook that security.

The Park Corner relatives turned to Maud often for financial help, as did other friends and family members. Of the many loans she made over the years, very few were ever paid back. Even the amiable treasurer of the Norval church "borrowed" church funds, and Maud covered the difference. She worked harder than ever at producing and selling stories. Maud began responding to fan letters by urging her admirers to tell her publishers how much they liked her work.

She also encouraged them to write to RKO Pictures about a favorite book—not *Anne of Green Gables,* of course, from whose films she knew she would never see a penny. But she was nonetheless delighted when, in 1934, a new, improved "talkie" version of *Anne of Green Gables* debuted. Maud made no profit from it, but she enjoyed the film. The actress who played Anne even changed her stage name to Anne Shirley, and reprised the role in a later film. Maud watched the new movie four times. When Maud wrote to George MacMillan about it, he replied he'd already seen the movie in Scotland—seven times!

Though critics favored more modern and experimental fiction, Maud's popularity among readers continued. A warm fan letter could save her day, bringing a welcome bit of light. But she often found herself pestered and pursued by strangers claiming to be relations or long-lost friends, demanding money, visits, and autographs. On Maud's rare visits home to Cavendish, she was badgered by people coming around to see "their" beloved author. They could not understand Maud's desire for privacy or for time alone with her family. She once wrote that "every freak" who had ever read *Anne of Green Gables* considered themselves her "kindred spirit." But one fan outdid them all—the eccentric and determined Isabel Anderson.

When Isabel first wrote, Maud assumed from Isabel's gushing style that she was a precocious young girl. Maud responded kindly. She was startled to discover that the fan who had expressed such schoolgirlish adoration was in fact a thirty-four-year-old teacher. But once Maud had written back encouragingly, Isabel Anderson could not be stopped. She plied Maud with letters, gifts, invitations, and phone calls. She would not let Maud rest till she had—somehow—managed to coax Maud into an overnight visit, all the while acting, Maud noted acidly, like "a blushing girl in the presence of her lover."

Isabel began coming to the Norval manse without invitation. She sulked and fumed when Maud did not respond, and even threatened suicide. A family friend remembered that during one unwelcome visit, Maud burst into the kitchen and announced in horror, "She wants to hold hands with me!" Maud eventually managed to shake off her stalker—who went on to pursue other objects of her affection with equal vigor.

True companionship was harder to find. Maud often turned to the consolation and company of her cats. Maud's much-adored Daffy had died years earlier, and Maud was heartbroken. "Get another cat," advised the unsympathetic Ewan. Maud didn't believe she could ever love another pet—till she met Good Luck, or Lucky, as he was called. Truly a cat with nine lives, Lucky survived a number of close calls—including a bout of double pneumonia.

Meanwhile, the vivacious and fun-loving Nora Lefurgey Campbell, Maud's great friend from years ago, moved nearby. Nora's visits were a delightful cure for loneliness. "Our minds seemed to strike sparks from each other," Maud enthused. She unearthed old photographs that Maud and Nora had taken, posing in bathing suits by the shore of Prince Edward Island. They teased and insulted each other, quoted from Shakespeare, or sat silently appreciating the glory of a "sunset sky of rose and dark gold." Another night, in the "little violet-blue hour," they spent two wordless hours absorbing the beauty of an apple orchard. Nora offered a much-needed respite from the anxieties of daily life.

In 1931, the Macdonalds learned that Chester had flunked out of his first year of engineering studies at the University of Toronto and had been asked to leave the program. Maud reacted hysterically, as she often did when misfortunes came upon her sons. She wept all the way home, tears soaking into the collar of her coat. She'd always had a tendency toward the dramatic and felt things keenly, but these characteristics had grown sharper over time. So, too, had her exaggerated pride and vanity—the twin curses of her life. Her worry over her sons bordered on obsession. When Chester failed at life, at work, and in his studies, Maud was convinced the whole world talked of nothing else.

As more troubling news of Chester reached Maud's ears, she wrote, "I have spent two days in hell. I cannot see how I am to go on living. I have suffered so dreadfully that I feel as if I were going insane. And I have had to keep up a face to the world when something in my soul was bleeding to death."

It was around this time that, according to Mary Rubio, Maud "set aside her journal for almost three years. From 1933 until 1936, Maud was able only to scribble rough notes of daily events." Her journal entries became hard to decode. Not until 1936 did Maud go back and pick up the broken thread of those lost years. In September 1933, she wrote merely, "another hideous thing has come and a new worry." She does not explain, but one may suppose it had to do again with Chester. His name had failed to appear on an exam pass list—an omission that was righted the next day. No one ever had quite the same power to touch Maud's deepest sympathy, or to wound her. "I feel," she wrote about her eldest son, "as if something in me has been hurt to death."

Stuart was training to be a doctor and was making waves as a young gymnast, winning the 1933 Canadian national title in junior gymnastics. But Maud barely took time to celebrate his triumphs. She fretted and fumed about his girlfriend, Joy Laird, a pretty and affectionate girl Stuart had first met in Norval.

To Maud, who had always written in her stories *against* parental interference in matters of the heart, Stuart's relationship came as "a new little gnawing worry." Maud did her utmost to kill the romance, writing her younger son a scolding letter and extracting from him a promise that he would end things with Joy. Small wonder that Maud wrote in her journal, "I haven't liked myself one day this week." Yet she seemed unable to control her own behavior.

Chester stunned the family in December 1933 when he revealed that he had secretly married one of his local girlfriends, the pregnant Luella Reid. Luella was by all accounts a "nice girl," devoted to her father and truly in love with Chester. But Chester was a minister's son, and an out-of-wedlock pregnancy was a serious matter. Chester claimed they had married a year earlier, in 1932. Ewan kept muttering over and over, "I don't believe a word of it." Of course Ewan was right. Chester was indeed lying. The young couple had married a week before they made their shocking announcement. Five and a half months later, Luella gave birth to a daughter, also named Luella.

Maud spent months bitterly digesting the news of the hasty marriage—and Luella's obvious pregnancy— but once little Luella was born, Maud fell in love with her brand-new granddaughter, whom she affectionately dubbed "Puss."

Maud had promised her daughter-in-law's late mother that she would watch over the motherless girl. She visited Toronto, where the young couple rented a three-bedroom apartment, and gave what she considered to be good advice. Her suggestions were wildly out-of-date. For instance, she told the pregnant Luella to install a dressing screen in the bedroom so that her husband would never see her naked. Maud kept such a screen in her own room. Luella didn't know whether to laugh or cry. Modesty was the least of her problems. Chester was an unfaithful and inattentive husband. After a few months of misery, Luella moved back to her father's house.

The clergyman in Ewan Macdonald saw all this as further proof that his sins had been visited on his first-born child. The presence of his little granddaughter left him stony-eyed. Maud commented, "In many ways Ewan is a very odd man, even when he is well, and never seems to have the reactions to anything that normal men have." Ewan discovered something wrong with his blood pressure and heart, and the terror of this news drove him into a depression even more severe than anything he had suffered to date. Maud had thought nothing could match that terrible year of 1919, but 1934 proved worse.

Ewan lost his ability to memorize sermons. He read shakily from written notes. One awful summer day, he broke down completely in the middle of the Sunday service. Maud drove him to the Homewood Mental Institution in Guelph. Both husband and wife desperately needed a respite—Ewan from the demands of his ministry, and Maud from the constant burden of caring for Ewan.

Luckily, Stuart came home that summer, and Maud had the company of her son and her affectionate cat, Lucky, plus occasional visits from her old pal Nora Lefurgey, to keep her from unraveling.

Still, Maud feared a total collapse. "This must not be. What would become of us all if I did?" Stuart had kept his promise not to marry Joy Laird, but it broke Joy's heart and his, and Maud found her youngest son uncharacteristically distant. When he kissed her, or made her some toast and tea, it was an event worthy of comment. Maud escaped into daydreams of the happy past, when both sons were small and their needs simple.

In this same period, her own creative gifts flagged. The loss of her "gift of wings" cannot have escaped her and was perhaps the cruelest blow of all. Maud published *Pat of Silver Bush* in 1933. Readers and critics have noted that Pat is one of Maud's few dull child heroines. Pat's main—some readers would say her *only*—characteristic is her neurotic, monotonous attachment to home, and her dread of "a terrible thing called change . . . and another terrible thing . . . disillusionment." These two elements—change and disillusionment—were fiercely at work in Maud's life. For once, she could not escape them in her art, nor transform them into fiction.

Ewan came home from the asylum only to fall victim to accidental poisoning the next day. The doctor had prescribed some "blue pills" for him, but instead of the usual tranquilizer, the druggist had grabbed a bottle of deadly pesticide. Ewan immediately began vomiting and suffering from stomach cramps. Only Maud's quick thinking saved him—and the fact that their local doctor happened to store the antidote to that particular poison.

Ewan survived the close call but staggered on in misery. He was unable to preach in September and October, and the church issued an ultimatum: the ailing minister had till December to regain his strength or resign. Ewan received electric shock therapy as well as his usual cocktail of sedatives, hypnotics, and sleeping pills. His memory was shattered. Among other remedies—some of them home-brewed—Ewan was now taking chloral, Veronal, Seconal, Medinal, Luminal, Nembutal, and tonics containing strychnine and arsenic. Maud was fond of something called "Chinese pills," which may have contained an opioid (similar to opium). Ewan walked around with a small bottle of alcohol-laced cough syrup in his pocket and drank from the bottle all day long.

In February 1935, a misunderstanding with the Norval church people triggered the inevitable. Ewan was called to a special session meeting on Valentine's Day in which, instead of being met with expressions of love, he was told that the local congregants "didn't want to come to church because of him." Luella Reid's father was one of the men who confronted him. Ewan was at his best in the face of an open conflict. He learned that a letter had gone out from Presbyterian main headquarters advising the local churches not to let the ministers' salaries fall behind. The congregants still felt sure that Ewan was the instigator. Hadn't they always paid him on time? Why was Ewan setting the higher authorities against them? They did not realize they had simply received a form letter, one sent to all congregations.

Even after the truth came out, hard feelings lingered.

The Norval congregation insisted that since Ewan could no longer perform his duties, it was time for him to leave. They had seen him driving around with his famous wife on days when he claimed to be too ill to preach. Certainly all the gossip about Chester's misdeeds had hurt Ewan's reputation as well. Ewan was sixty-five, sick, depressed, and exhausted. He was done fighting.

Years earlier, Maud and Ewan had gone together to see a beautiful, tragic movie called *Journey's End,* a war film about a man at the edge of a breakdown. Maud loved the film, yet found it so sad she could hardly bear to watch it to its conclusion. Once the Macdonalds determined to move from Norval, they settled on a neighborhood in the West End of Toronto and fell in love with a home on Riverside Drive. It was an expensive house, but Maud made the down payment and took on the mortgage. Here at long last was not a church manse that could be taken away from them, but a proper home, "the house of her dreams." Prophetically, Maud named the place Journey's End.

Journey's End

Nearly everyone who hears the story of Maud Montgomery asks the same question: Why didn't she return to Prince Edward Island when at last she was free to go wherever she pleased? On a visit back in 1929, she wrote, "here only am I a complete being. . . . I never should have left it." One can't help wondering what would have happened if she had left Norval and gone home. Maud, too, played at what-ifs. She wondered in her journal, what if she had gone to Lower Bedeque before she or Herman Leard were engaged to others? What if *Anne of Green Gables* had been published earlier—would she have accepted Ewan's proposal? What if Ewan had stayed on in Cavendish and they'd never left Prince Edward Island?

Of course, Cavendish, too, had changed over time. By 1935, there was no longer even a Presbyterian church in town — the local church had gone United, a fact particularly wounding to Maud. The beloved old Macneill homestead had been torn down by Uncle John in 1920.

As a final transformation, the Canadian government bought the farmhouse that had once belonged to Maud's cousins David and Margaret Macneill — the famous house on which Green Gables was loosely based. Cavendish had become a popular destination for fans wanting to visit places they had read about in *Anne of Green Gables*. Now the government created a national park around the Macneill house. The magnificent park, forty kilometers long, contains beaches and dunes, spruce groves, Lover's Lane, and the Haunted Wood.

It was a year of exceptional honors. Maud was made a member of the OBE, an officer of the Order of the British Empire. Officially, she declared herself honored to have her work recognized by the government, happy that an authentic Prince Edward Island farmhouse would be preserved and the lands protected. At a more personal level, she was sorry to lose property that had long belonged to her family.

In a strange way, the creation of the national park preserved the island's connection with Maud's work at the same instant that it severed her personal ties. Much on the island had changed beyond recognition. Beloved people and places were gone. Maud had memorialized them in dozens of beautiful books, in hundreds of stories and poems. Now she could only put her face to the future and hope for the best.

Shortly before leaving the Norval manse, Maud had a dream of her Cavendish home. On the verge of what would be her final move, she dreamed:

> *I was home again in my dear old room in Cavendish. I seemed to know that I was going to stay there. It was clean and fresh with a nice new window in it. The furniture was strewn about and parcels were lying everywhere but I thought, "I can soon bring everything into order and have my own dear room again." Grandma was there, too, smiling and kind.*

Maud thought optimistically about the dream. It was a sign, she thought, that they were soon going to find a house that they could all love. Shortly after, she and Ewan spied a For Sale sign outside a house on Riverside Drive with tall pine trees behind it. The pines were enough to make her look twice. The house boasted a fireplace in the living room, and another in the recreation-room area of the basement. There was a beautiful casement window in the dining room, a large master bedroom with a walk-in closet, and a glimpse of the lake. "I knew I must have the house. What a place for cats to prowl in!"

Despite Maud's wounded pride at the way they were forced to leave Norval, she had something new to look forward to. And she would write *Jane of Lantern Hill* here — one of her few novels set outside of Prince Edward Island. Much of the story takes place in a neighborhood of Toronto like that of Journey's End. Jane, the book's young heroine, feels torn between her two parents and their two ways of life — one urban and sophisticated, the other seaside and rural. The book evokes the delights of both Toronto and Prince Edward Island; it is arguably L. M. Montgomery's last masterwork, a novel of fairy-tale beauty, longing, and deft lightness.

Maud's capacity for love extended to people, places, landscapes, and animals — and among animals, cats reigned supreme. Just before the book's publication, Maud's favorite cat, Lucky, died. For Maud, it was more than the simple loss of a pet — she had lost her most trusted companion. She grieved for Lucky as she had not grieved in years. In fact, she dedicated *Jane of Lantern Hill* "to the memory of 'LUCKY' the charming affectionate comrade of fourteen years."

Maud had counted all her life on a handful of loved ones whose presence reliably lightened and brightened her days: her father; Will Pritchard; Frede; her youngest son, Stuart; and the cat Lucky. Now only Stuart remained.

Maud fumed and worried about Stuart's long-standing connection to Joy Laird, and against her own better instincts, she continued to meddle in her son's affairs. She was delighted when he began dating a new girl, Margaret, in Toronto — and deeply chagrined when Margaret's parents intervened to break up the romance. Margaret's mother privately called the Macdonald household that "crazy house."

They had good reason to worry about the Macdonalds. Chester continued to behave in ways that would have horrified any proper middle-class family. Retired now, cast off from daily work, and at loose ends, Ewan shambled around Journey's End looking ill and unkempt.

Stuart conducted medical tests and found his father's system dangerously taxed by all the medication he took. Ewan's reckless combination of drugs had inflicted damage. Normally a peaceful man, he could become irascible, even violent. He once aimed a gun at Nora Lefurgey's head, then tried to pass it off as a joke.

Chester, the prodigal elder son, continued to behave disgracefully — chasing women and neglecting his wife and child, his studies, and his job. He could be charming when he chose. But he had a dark side as well. Maud knew that something had to be done to control her eldest son — but what? Her pleas, threats, and earnest talks all failed equally.

Chester dropped out of engineering school to study law. His employer fired him for negligence and only took him back after pleas and promises from Maud. Chester and Luella had another child in 1936, a son named Cameron Craig Stuart, but Luella did not move back in, and Chester seemed just as glad to live without a wife and children tying him down.

He began a long-term affair with a local woman. His daily behavior became more erratic. When his spirits were high, Chester gadded about, dating several women at once, chasing others, and taking parts in hammy theatricals. When Maud moved to Toronto, Chester's employer remarked that he was glad she was moving close by. "You will be able to keep check on Chester." It stung her pride, yet she knew her eldest son was out of control.

In January 1937, Maud found and read part of Chester's diary. We don't know what she discovered, but it finally destroyed her trust in her eldest son. She wrote, "On that day all happiness departed from my life forever. . . . It cannot be written or told—that unspeakable horror. Oh God, can I ever forget that day? Not in eternity." Whatever she learned created "one of the most dreadful situations a woman could be placed in."

Maud feared Chester must be insane. She hinted at dark secrets haunting the family. Had someone tried to blackmail them? We cannot know for sure, but in March, Maud was released from the worst of her anxieties. She had come into unexpected income from one of her investments—perhaps it was enough to buy Chester's way out of his troubles.

Maud changed the terms of her will so that Chester would inherit nothing—not even personal items—unless he was living with Luella at the time of Maud's death. Marriage and fatherhood, Maud hoped, might stabilize his life. She arranged for Stuart to be executor of her affairs, since Ewan was in no condition to look after anything.

When one of Ewan's chronic headaches struck, he tied up his head in a handkerchief —an ominous sign of long, ghastly hours ahead. Now Ewan sometimes lurched around the house with a hot-water bottle tied to his head. Since he was mixing barbiturates, bromides, tranquilizers, and alcohol, as well as other mystery and herbal pills, it's a wonder he could stand at all.

In 1937, Ewan was invited to preach to his old congregation in Leaskdale. He was understandably anxious about going, but Maud insisted. When he told her he felt he was dying, she gave him smelling salts and sat him in the driver's seat. Thus began one of the worst public nightmares of their life. By the time they reached the Leaskdale church, Ewan could no longer speak. He mumbled incoherently into the pulpit for a few minutes and then, in dazed confusion, sat back down. The congregation was kind, reassuring Maud that it had been good just to "hear his voice again." They undoubtedly thought Ewan in some final stages of senility. On the drive home to Toronto, he lost his way, driving around and around in hopeless circles, and twice landed the car in a ditch. In the end, Maud and Ewan spent the night shivering at the side of the road, too frightened to drive the rest of the way home.

Maud had long invented stories about her own life. But the story she now told herself was darkness and despair: in her words, "hell, hell, hell." The journal, her trusty grumble book, became a record of howling anguish. Each year was the "worst year"—in 1924, in 1937, and again in 1940–1941. Confession didn't ease the pain. For the first time, Maud's storytelling—at least as reflected in her journals—only made things worse.

It's almost unimaginable that Maud remained as prolific as she did in this final, terrible period of her life. Yet she wrote a sequel to *Pat of Silverbush,* and began her final Anne book, *Anne of Ingleside,* in the spring of 1937. She worked on it all fall and finished it—her twenty-first book, she noted proudly—that same December.

Anne of Ingleside takes us back to the happy period when Anne's children are still growing and having innocent adventures. The novel features the difficult, comic, and ever-complaining Aunt Mary Maria. Maud reveals a resurgence of her old fiery imagination in *Anne of Ingleside.* Eccentric characters step forward to take their star turns, and Anne, Gilbert, and their children feel like fully realized characters.

In Ingleside, Anne moves into her own as a

full-grown woman and mother. She is no longer the innocent, wide-eyed child. "Anne shivered. Motherhood was very sweet . . . but very terrible. 'I wonder what life holds for them,' she whispered." The book reflects some of Maud's own hard-earned life lessons: "Well, that was life. Gladness and pain . . . hope and fear . . . and change. Always change! You could not help it. You had to let the old go and take the new to your heart. . . . Spring, lovely as it was, must yield to summer and summer lose itself in autumn."

Maud wrote not just these books but a host of shorter pieces. In this same dark period, she composed a lively article about her favorite books, and sent countless letters of encouragement to young writers. Even in the depths of despair, she reached out to aspiring artists. Younger Canadian writers remember Montgomery as a kind and consistent mentor, always willing to help, edit, and introduce. She spared herself no time or trouble on behalf of others.

Ironically, just as her creative powers were returning, Maud witnessed a further drop in her literary standing. She was edged out of the executive committee of the Canadian Authors Association. That wounded her pride and made her feel as she had in her isolated youth, an outlier living in a remote province. *Mistress Pat,* a sequel, was rejected by Hodder & Stoughton, the same company that had published *Pat of Silver Bush*. It had been a long time since Maud had experienced flat-out editorial dismissal. She went with a smaller company, Harrap. *Mistress Pat* proved to be a popular success. Later, when Hodder & Stoughton wrote to ask their spurned author for her next book, she turned them down flat. Maud did not easily forgive or forget a slight.

On April 17, 1939, Maud began a sequel to *Jane of Lantern Hill*, tentatively titled *Jane and Jody*. Writing was both a relief and a sign of renewed energy. Maud made a last visit home to Prince Edward Island that spring. As always on these visits, her mood became more buoyant, her handwriting less shaky. Like the mythical Antaeus whose mother is Earth, as soon as Maud's feet touched home ground, her strength was renewed. But she soon turned to Journey's End in Toronto, drawn by duty to Ewan and the life that was killing her. So quick to rescue others, both in fiction and in life, Maud failed in the end to rescue herself.

The errant Chester moved in for a time with Luella and the children, in Aurora, a town just north of Toronto. Maud paid for him to buy a share of a legal firm with a lawyer named Downey. But his return home did not mean that Chester had become a dutiful and loving husband and father—far from it.

Chester stayed out till all hours. He neglected his

young family, failing to provide even the most basic comforts. Luella dressed the children in clothing remade from Maud's hand-me-downs, and she heated the kitchen—the one livable room in the house—with firewood she salvaged and chopped herself. Chester ate breakfast at home—the only meal he ate with family—wearing his heavy coat and gloves against the freezing cold. The children huddled around the kitchen fire. Still Luella hung on, determined to make the marriage work. Then she visited her doctor, only to learn that Chester had given her a venereal disease. This was the last straw. Luella took the children home to live with her father. Chester slunk to Journey's End in disgrace and moved into his parents' basement.

There was one bright note in 1939. Anita Webb, Maud's distant relation from Prince Edward Island, came to join the family in June. Anita became an invaluable helper and welcome companion with her sturdy, sunny disposition. Anita and Maud worked well together at simple chores—Anita washing the dishes, Maud drying them. They shopped together once a week at the local store and the butcher's. Anita was fiercely protective of Maud and disliked Chester, who she felt cheated and bullied Maud. One day he "borrowed" his mother's expensive Kodak movie camera, only to report it "stolen" the next day.

By September 1939, war was declared again in Europe.

Maud watched the growing conflict with dread. She had suffered through World War I, trembling at each setback, dreaming of the war each night. She had seen the sufferings of friends and family who lost loved ones.

Now the danger edged closer to home. Maud's two sons were of age to fight. Chester registered for military service but was rejected because of poor eyesight. Stuart had set his heart on the navy, and planned to enlist as soon as his medical internship ended.

Maud did not believe she could survive a second world war. Horrified, she watched Hitler make inroads through Europe. "A madman is in control," she declared. She saw the world as "riding on an avalanche." In this dire state of mind, she felt certain that Stuart would be killed. "I have seen all my other hopes crushed to death," she wrote in her journal. "Why should this one survive?" Maud's despair deepened on all fronts. Ewan's health and state of mind were as fragile as her own. He tried "a new medicine every day and nothing has the slightest effect."

Perhaps most devastating of all, Maud's ability to express herself in words had finally deserted her entirely. This was the ultimate blow to a mind that had always been lit by radiant imagination. Biographers Mary Rubio and Elizabeth Waterston have suggested that "true tragedy came into her life when she could no longer write — neither fiction nor fixative journals."

In 1940, Maud fell and injured her right arm. A few

years earlier she had hurt her left arm but was thankful at least that she still had the use of her good arm. Now she could barely perform even basic household tasks. She could write only a few words at a time. Maud had trouble sleeping, and believed that she would never get well, though her local doctor, Dr. Lane, tried to convince her otherwise. She wrote to her ever-loyal friend George MacMillan, "I do not ask you to write me until you hear that I am better." Yet his cheerful "sane letter" raised her spirits considerably, and she read his soothing words over and over.

Chester had become an expert at manipulating his mother to get what he wanted. "He was always after money," Anita Webb reported grimly. Chester now became the affectionate child, Stuart the more reserved. Maids would find Chester in Maud's bedroom, lying with his head on her shoulder, while she ran her fingers through his dark hair. There is an eerie resemblance here to her passionate evenings with Herman Leard. When Chester needed the car to drive around town trolling for women, he came to Maud in his most winning mode. Other times—for instance, when he needed money quickly—he would become aggressive, angry, and bullying.

Maud grew tremulous and frightened, nearly unrecognizable from her usual upright and energetic self. "My conception of heaven," she wrote in her journal, "would be life without fear." Maud clung to Anita Webb like a child, following her from room to room. Yet in this same period she remained a poised and popular public speaker, full of funny, lively, sparkling stories. Anita was struck by the stark difference between these two Mauds, the public and the private woman.

Then, in early 1942, family problems forced Anita to travel home to Cavendish for a long visit. Stuart arranged for a temporary nurse to look after Maud. In this period, Maud could barely express herself coherently. Her journal entries are few and agonized. The hired nurse wrote to fans and friends explaining that Maud was too ill to correspond. Her final postcards to her old pen pals Weber and MacMillan sound alarmingly distraught. In her last correspondence to MacMillan, she confessed:

> *The past year has been one of constant blows to me. My eldest son has made a mess of his life, and his wife has left him. My husband's nerves are worse than mine even. I have kept the nature of his attacks from you for over 20 years but they have broken me at last. . . . I expect conscription will come in and they will take my second son and then I will give up all effort to recover because I shall have nothing to live for.*

The word that comes up again and again is *broken.* Broken heart, broken spirit, broken down: a "dread that I am going to break down altogether." Maud was still keeping notes toward her journal, but she no longer had the strength to gather them into a coherent narrative. As she had done during the terrible mid-1930s, she would write up rough notes, planning to later edit them and make the narrative more flowing, using these notes to reconstruct her days. By mid-April she had compiled 175 pages of those rough notes.

In spring, Anita Webb returned at last from Prince Edward Island, and her calm presence was a blessing, but Maud continued her relentless downward spiral. Her last known act is a literary one. On April 23 she took in hand her newest book, a story collection called *The Blythes Are Quoted,* and mailed the manuscript off to her publisher.

The Blythes Are Quoted is a complex, divided book — one half taking place before World War I, one half after. It is one of Montgomery's most experimental books, a fictional collage consisting of snippets of a novelistic narrative, stand-alone stories, descriptive passages, and poems. To the very end, Maud was stretching and testing herself as an artist.

On the morning of April 24, 1942, Dr. Lane phoned Stuart at his office with terrible news. Anita Webb had found Maud in her bed, a bottle of pills lying beside her. There was no way to revive her. Stuart came to the house at once. On the table by her bed lay a piece of writing dated a few days earlier. It was numbered page 176 and written in legible and flowing handwriting. It reads as follows, beginning calmly enough:

> *This copy is unfinished and never will be. It is in a terrible state because I made it when I had begun to suffer my terrible breakdown of 1942. It must end here. If any publishers wish to publish extracts from it under the terms of my will they must stop here. The tenth volume can never be copied and must not be made public during my lifetime. Parts of it are too terrible and would hurt people.*

The passage continues, increasingly desperate in tone:

> *I have lost my mind by spells and I do not dare to think what I may do in those spells. May God forgive me and I hope everyone will forgive me even if they cannot understand. My position is too awful to endure and nobody realizes it. What an end to a life in which I tried always to do my best in spite of many mistakes.*

Stuart and Dr. Lane believed what they found by Maud's bed was a suicide note. Neither man was aware that Maud used rough notes like these to compose her journal, and they did not stop to consider the date, nor the fact that the page was numbered page 176. Stuart hastily shoved the paper into his pocket. Dr. Lane advised Stuart

314

to look after Maud's personal effects while he wrote up the report for the coroner.

The scandal over Maud's apparent suicide would have been enormous, so the family decided to guard their secret. In that regard, not much has changed in the last seventy-five years. Suicides are even now considered shameful, private matters. Stuart kept the folded note to himself and said nothing further about it for more than fifty years. Dr. Lane's own reputation was on the line as well. After all, Lane had prescribed the medication that had killed his patient. No one openly discussed the bedside note for decades.

Finally, in September 2008, the Macdonald family broke their silence. Stuart's daughter, Kate Macdonald Butler, came forward with the family's permission to declare Maud's death a suicide, and to describe her grandmother's long struggle against depression. "I have come to feel very strongly that the stigma surrounding mental illness will be forever upon us as a society until we sweep away the misconception that depression happens to other people, not us — and most certainly not to our heroes and icons," Kate wrote.

At the time of Maud's death, the coroner's report declared the death a result of "arteriosclerosis and a very high degree of neurasthenia." (*Neurasthenia* is a term that covers a wide range of psychological and nerve disorders.) Experts and fans have been debating the circumstances of L. M. Montgomery's tragic death ever since. And there is reason to feel uncertain.

Maud regularly mixed enough medications to kill a much stronger woman. She had lost a great deal of weight quickly, and may not have realized that a dose that seemed right at her usual weight would be lethal in her present condition. Maud's death by overdose may have been an accident, or it may have been deliberate. She wrote in her journal, "The present is unbearable. The past is spoiled. There is no future." Her despair was clear. Nor did Maud believe that suicide was a sin. Decades earlier, she had noted: "My attitude to it is much that which I have found quoted in Lecky. 'Life is forced on us; we did not ask for it; therefore, it if becomes too hard we have a right to lay it down.'"

After a minor surgery, she once came out of the anesthesia saying, "Oh, doctor, heaven is so beautiful I'm sorry you called me back." She had been toying with the idea of death, thinking about it for a long time. One young visitor shortly before the end was told that Maud did not "expect to be there" in a week or so. That statement mystified the young friend. It is no mystery that Maud was sad enough to die.

Other puzzles remain unsolved. For instance, what happened to the other 175 rough pages of her journal notes? They might shed more light on the circumstances of Maud's final days. But those pages disappeared around the time of her death and have never resurfaced. Likely they were deliberately destroyed. Undoubtedly they contained passages that would have been especially damning to Chester.

We know that Chester began removing things from the house almost as soon as Maud's body was discovered. Chester's later life was full of troubles and petty crimes — he was jailed for embezzlement, and he died in his early fifties, of unknown and suspicious causes. According to the terms of the will, since Chester was no longer living with Luella, he had no rights to any personal property. Yet he kept taking carloads of things out of the house, till neighbors finally called the estate, and the locks on the house were changed.

Living in the basement of Journey's End, Chester probably had greatest access to Maud's habits and hiding places. He was out of the house when Maud's body was found. But he would have had sufficient time later to dispose of all but her final note.

Maud had once specified the epitaph she wanted on Frede's gravestone. "After life's fitful fever she sleeps well." She added, "It is the one I want on my own when I die. And I trust I shall sleep well . . . For I think it will take me a long while to get rested."

Maud's body was flown to Prince Edward Island for burial beside her relatives. She once wrote that any visitor to her island must feel "I have come home." There, she declared, "we realize that eternity exists . . . 'our own will come to us'—we have only to wait." Maud's body lay in state at the house known as Green Gables, and was driven to the Cavendish church for the funeral on April 29, 1942. The local outpouring of grief was immense. The little white wooden church filled to over-flowing. Mourners spilled out of the church and onto the grounds. The Cavendish school closed for the after-noon; grieving schoolchildren came running over. One girl remembered telling her mother, "I have read all her books and I know her."

Ewan Macdonald, the widower, was bewildered and disoriented. Maud's death struck a terrible blow to his sense of reality. He kept wandering off during the funeral, calling, "Poor Maud, poor Maud," like a bird without its mate. At other moments his voice interrupted the cer-emony, crying out, "Who is dead? Who is dead?" Then he would call in a ringing voice, "Who is she? Too bad! Too bad!"

John Sterling, Ewan's old friend, the minister who had presided at their marriage service, conducted Maud's funeral. He spoke of her personal and artistic accomplish-ments, predicting that future generations would "feel their pulses quicken at the thought of their proximity to the dust of one who painted life so joyously, so full of hope, and of sweetness and light."

On the day of Maud's funeral, spring had not yet arrived on Prince Edward Island. The temperatures that late April day hovered near freezing. Snow lay in drifts along the ground. When John Sterling gave his eulogy, a warm island wind blew over the gathered mourners. The day briefly brightened. The birds of spring sang their first notes. Maud had come home at last.

EPILOGUE

The teenage Maud who ruefully confided to her journal "I have no influence of any kind in any quarter" touched millions of readers with her words. And the young writer who jubilantly celebrated her first five-dollar check became one of the best-paid authors of her time. Maud feared she would always live in poverty, in rented rooms; instead she lived to buy a house she loved in an elegant neighborhood of Toronto. Scolded as a child for indulging her peculiar habit of "scribbling," she became one of the most important Canadian writers the world has known.

The popularity of L. M. Montgomery's writing continues unabated. Maud's books have sold millions of copies.

Her work lives on in dozens of forms—some of which she never knew, and could not have even imagined. Her writing has been successfully adapted to the stage, the movies, and for television, and is available in books, CDs, and DVDs. Discussions of her work abound in journals dedicated to her writings, and in online blogs and articles.

Anne's House of Dreams was distributed to Polish soldiers during World War II to lend them courage and hope. Her words have been read and memorized by countless fans of all ages, cultures, and backgrounds. One young girl, confined by illness to her bed, confided that she had read *Anne of Green Gables* more than fifteen times. It may be the most *reread* of all children's novels.

Thousands of visitors flock to Prince Edward Island each summer to pay homage to L. M. Montgomery and her work. The late author is the best-known national treasure of her island home. Prince Edward Island estimates that 350,000 come to visit Green Gables each year. Kate Middleton, as the newlywed wife of Prince William, flew to Prince Edward Island on her honeymoon in honor of the book, citing Montgomery as one of her favorite and most influential authors.

Kate Middleton was not Green Gables's first famous visitor, nor will she be the last. In 1927, Stanley Baldwin, then prime minister of England, wrote a fan letter to Maud, asking if she would be on Prince Edward Island when he came to visit. "It would give me keen pleasure to have an opportunity of shaking your hand and thanking you for the pleasure your books have given me. . . . I must see Green Gables before I return home."

Maud read that letter while strolling in her beloved Lover's Lane, marveling that such a note had come the way of "the little girl who walked here years ago and dreamed—and wrote her dreams into books." She had expected little by way of success—she had been raised to expect nothing at all. To many of her childhood friends and neighbors, she seemed a mere charity case. Yet a British prime minister flew all the way to her remote island to meet her.

Maud's books and dreams live on. Her works are treasured by children and adults all over the world—they are particular favorites among Japanese schoolchildren, fellow islanders living half a world away. Her work has taken on as many forms as it's possible to imagine—animation, comic books, radio shows, magazines, movies and theatrical presentations. The musical *Anne of Green Gables* played in England, Africa, Asia, and America and has been performed to full houses in Charlottetown, Prince Edward Island, for more than forty-five years.

The 1986 television miniseries *Anne of Green Gables* won an Emmy Award and swept television's other honors, making still more popular Maud's already well-known books. Two award-winning television movies followed, and then a successful television series called *The Road to*

Avonlea. Anne with an E aired this year, offering a darker vision of her work. Her single most beloved and famous book, *Anne of Green Gables,* has sold more than fifty million copies worldwide and been translated into more than twenty languages.

Maud bequeathed her readers thousands of pages of beautiful writing—novels and stories, memoir, poetry, biography, and vignettes. She left behind thousands of pages of her journals, and hundreds of pages of lively letters. Her private writings are often as gorgeous as her published works. The wonder is not that L. M. Montgomery struggled, but that she rose above her suffering for so long and accomplished so much in the face of it. As she tried to explain to one young fan, fame and success were no guarantee against life's sorrows. "What . . . can fence out the cares and problems that enter into all lives?"

Maud suffered from chronic depression, and likely also from bouts of manic depression, yet she produced twenty novels and hundreds of short stories, even in her most difficult and desperate years. Writing for her was not merely a hobby, it was a way of life, a constantly renewed and renewing way of seeing the world. She was a noted speaker, a popular teacher, a pioneering newspaperwoman, an accomplished craftswoman, a capable homemaker, a world traveler, and a brilliant writer.

In *Anne of Green Gables,* she transformed her personal story of abandonment into a glorious tale of love and rescue. Often sad, Maud provided laughter and joy for others. She was passionately loving and passionately beloved. Her friendships were deep and enduring. She, who married late and feared she would never have any sort of domestic happiness, raised two sons. She witnessed snowstorms and sun showers, sunrises and new moons she claimed she would "remember even into the halls of eternity." Maud found life beautiful: to the very end, there were things to marvel at and to love. "Perfect happiness I have never had—never will have," she confided to her journal. "Yet there have been, after all, many wonderful and exquisite hours in my life."

Time Line of L. M. Montgomery's Life

1874
Born November 30, Clifton, Prince Edward Island,
to Hugh John and Clara Macneill Montgomery

1876
Mother dies of tuberculosis

1883
The Nelson boys come to live with the Macneills.
Wreck of the ship the *Marco Polo* near Cavendish

1890–1891
Trip to Prince Albert, Saskatchewan, to visit her father and
his new wife and child. Maud destroys old journals and
begins new. First publication, in Saskatchewan newspaper,
"proudest day of my life"

1893–1894
Attends Prince of Wales College and earns
first class teacher's license

1894–1895
Teaches school in Bideford, PEI

1895–1896
Attends Dalhousie University in Halifax.
Receives first payment for her writings, a five-dollar check

1896–1897
Teaches in Belmont, PEI, and becomes engaged
to her cousin Edwin Simpson

1897–1898
Teaches in Lower Bedeque, PEI; falls in love with
Herman Leard; breaks off engagement to Simpson.
Returns to Cavendish to live with Grandmother Macneill
when Grandfather Macneill dies

1901–1902
Works as newspaperwoman at *Daily Echo* in Halifax

1903
Ewan Macdonald begins as Presbyterian minister in Cavendish;
Maud starts her lifelong correspondence with George Boyd
MacMillan and Ephraim Weber

1906
Secretly engaged to Ewan Macdonald, who leaves to study in
Scotland and suffers nervous breakdown

1908
Publication of *Anne of Green Gables*

1909
Anne of Avonlea; Ewan Macdonald accepts parish in
Leaskdale, Ontario

1910
Kilmeny of the Orchard; Maud meets Earl and Lady Grey
in September; in November travels to Boston to meet
her publisher, L. C. Page & Company

1911

The Story Girl; Grandmother Macneill dies; Maud marries
Ewan Macdonald at Park Corner on July 5;
honeymoons in Scotland and England for three months;
home to Leaskdale, Ontario, in September

1912

Chronicles of Avonlea; her eldest son, Chester Cameron,
born July 7

1913

The Golden Road; trip to PEI

1914

First World War is declared; second child, Hugh Alexander,
stillborn on August 13

1915

Anne of the Island; Ewan Stuart born October 7

1916

The Watchman and Other Poems

1917

Anne's House of Dreams

1918

First World War ends; Maud suffers Spanish flu; goes to
PEI to help nurse sick relatives at Park Corner

1919

"A hellish year." Frede Campbell Macfarlane dies of Spanish flu in Montreal; Ewan suffers a nervous breakdown; *Rainbow Valley;* Maud sells all rights for *Anne of Green Gables* to Page, who immediately sells movie rights

1920

Further Chronicles of Avonlea published illegally; Maud begins eight-year lawsuit with Page & Co.; *Rilla of Ingleside*

1922

Car accident in Zephyr; Ewan is sued and goes to court; summer trip to Muskoka

1923

Emily of New Moon; Maud is first Canadian woman to become Fellow of the Royal Society of Arts in Britain

1925

Emily Climbs; church union vote passes in Canada

1926

The Blue Castle; move to Norval, Ontario

1927

Emily's Quest; Maud is presented to the Prince of Wales

1929

Magic for Marigold; stock market crash affects Maud's finances

1930

Goes to Prince Albert to rekindle friendships of 1890

1931

A Tangled Web

1933

Pat of Silver Bush

1934

Chester and Luella's baby Luella is born; *Courageous Women,*
Maud's first foray into biography

1935

Mistress Pat; Maud elected to Literary and Artistic Institute of
France; moves to Riverside Drive, Toronto (Journey's End);
is made Officer of the Order of the British Empire

1936

Anne of Windy Poplars; Cavendish chosen as site for
national park on Prince Edward Island

1937

Green Gables national site opens in Cavendish;
Jane of Lantern Hill

1939

Anne of Ingleside; Maud's last visit to PEI

1942

Dies on April 24; lies in state at Green Gables and
is buried in Cavendish Cemetery (where Ewan Macdonald
joins her one year later)

Source Notes

Chapter Two: An Early Sorrow

p. 16: "I loved my father . . . ever knew": Bolger and Epperly, p. 160.

Chapter Three: "Very Near to a Kingdom of Ideal Beauty"

p. 26: "If I believe . . . stage of existence": Ibid., p. 26.

Chapter Six: Count Nine Stars

p. 60: "very different indeed . . . my outward being": Ibid, p. 16.

Chapter Seven: "Darling Father" and Prince Albert

p. 79: "Then whisper . . . humble name": "The Fringed Gentian." *Godey's Lady's Book,* 1884, vol. 108, p. 237.

p. 83: "No decent father . . . such a trip alone": Rubio, p. 67.

Chapter Fourteen: Back in the House of Dreams

p. 168: "This morning we . . . shall stop short": Ibid., p. 112.

p. 171: "I gazed always . . . moonlight, sunset": Montgomery, "The Gay Days of Old," p. 46.

Chapter Fifteen: The Creation of Anne

p. 181: "having 'thought out' . . . my household work": Gammel, p. 148.

p. 183: "I can never be a really great writer": Bolger and Epperly, p. 21.

p. 183: "I think we . . . reach its own": Ibid., p. 9

p. 183: "a wide green . . . there are Junes": Ibid.

p. 192: "the dearest . . . immortal Alice": Andronik, p. 82.

pp. 192–193: "I don't think . . . of her name": Bolger and Epperly, p. 41.

Chapter Sixteen: "Yes, I Understand the Young Lady Is a Writer"

p. 202: "a bilious headache": Ibid., p. 52.

p. 206: "Sleet blew . . . whole way home": Gammel, p. 248.

p. 210: "If two people . . . would be excellent": Bolger and Epperly, p. 32.

p. 212: "Color is . . . it is a passion": Ibid., p. 13.

Chapter Twenty: Dashing over the Traces

p. 225: "Those whom the gods . . . ministers' wives": Rubio and Waterston, vol. 2, p. xiii.

p. 227: "I like Leaskdale . . . I do not love it": Bolger and Epperly, p. 65.

p. 235: "It seemed passionately . . . leave it again": Ibid., p. 68.

p. 240: "All the sorrow . . . equal it in agony": Ibid., p. 71.

p. 241: "not had one decent dinner since the war began": Ibid.

p. 267: "I swear it as a dark and deadly vow": Rubio, p. 289.

p. 268: "I can't afford . . . cater to it for awhile": Bolger and Epperly, p. 119.

p. 271: "dreamed it all out . . . September": Ibid., p. 109.

p. 276: "I content myself . . . turn a corner": Ibid., p. 85.

p. 276: "Ewan was maladroit . . . practical or mechanical . . . Whoa!": Rubio, p. 238.

p. 280: "made unhappy . . . in our church": Bolger and Epperly, p. 127.

p. 281: "it is one of the beauty spots of Ontario": Ibid., p. 127.

p. 283: "Sometimes I get . . . go to another": Ibid., p. 137.

p. 290: "set aside . . . of daily events": Rubio and Waterston, *Selected Journals,* vol. 4, p. xv.

p. 296: "the house of her dreams": Rubio, p. 444.

Chapter Twenty-One: Journey's End

p. 310: "true tragedy . . . nor fixative journals": Rubio and Waterston, *Writing a Life,* p. 116.

p. 311: "I do not ask . . . I am better": Bolger and Epperly, p. 201.

p. 311: "He was always after money": Rubio, p. 565.

p. 312: "The past year . . . to live for": Bolger and Epperly, p. 204.

p. 315: "arteriosclerosis and . . . neurasthenia": Rubio, p. 585.

p. 316: "My attitude . . . lay it down'": Tiessen and Tiessen, p. 105.

p. 318: "I have read all her books and I know her": Heilbron and McCabe, p. 6.

p. 318: "'Poor Maud' . . . 'Too bad!'": Rubio, p. 584.

p. 318: "feel their pulses . . . sweetness and light": Ibid.

EPILOGUE
p. 324: "What . . . can fence . . . into all lives?": Ibid.

Bibliography

Andronik, Catherine M. *Kindred Spirit*. New York: Atheneum Books for Young Readers, 1993.

Bolger, Francis W. P. *The Years Before Anne*. Prince Edward Island Heritage Foundation, 1974.

Bolger, Francis W. P., and Elizabeth R. Epperly, eds. *My Dear Mr. M: Letters to G. B. MacMillan from L. M. Montgomery*. Toronto: Oxford University Press, 1992.

Eggleston, Wilfrid, ed. *The Green Gables Letters: From L. M. Montgomery to Ephraim Weber, 1905–1909*. Toronto: Ryerson Press, 1960.

Gammel, Irene. *Looking for Anne of Green Gables*. New York: St. Martin's Press, 2008.

Heilbron, Alexandra, and Kevin McCabe, eds. *The Lucy Maud Montgomery Album*. Toronto: Fitzhenry & Whiteside, 1999.

Montgomery, L. M. "The Alpine Path: The Story of My Career." Pts. 1–6. *Everywoman's World,* June–November, 1917.

———. "The Gay Days of Old." *Farmers' Magazine* 18 (December 15, 1919): 46.

Rubio, Mary Henley. *Lucy Maud Montgomery: A Gift of Wings*. Toronto: Doubleday Canada, 2008.

Rubio, Mary, and Elizabeth Waterston, eds. *The Selected Journals of L. M. Montgomery*. 5 vols. Toronto: Oxford University Press, 1985–2004.

Rubio, Mary, and Elizabeth Waterston. *Writing a Life: L. M. Montgomery*. Toronto: ECW Press, 1995.

Simpson, Harold H. *Cavendish: Its History, Its People, Its Founding Families.* Amherst, NS: Harold H. Simpson & Associates, 1973.

Tiessen, Hildi Froese, and Paul Gerard Tiessen, eds. *After Green Gables: L. M. Montgomery's Letters to Ephraim Weber, 1916–1941.* Toronto: University of Toronto Press, 2006.

In addition, the L. M. Montgomery Research Centre at the University of Guelph made available to me countless useful notebooks, daybooks, letters, articles, and artifacts—including samples of Maud's own exquisite needlework and the famous spotted china dogs she purchased on her honeymoon. All uncited quotes come from Maud's unpublished personal journals or from her published memoir, "The Alpine Path: The Story of My Career."

There are many fine websites dedicated to the life and work of L. M. Montgomery. Among the most useful to young scholars is the L. M. Montgomery Literary Society, which is always publishing new articles on various aspects of her biography, friends, relations, and work. They may be found at http://lmmontgomeryliterarysociety.weebly.com/.

Acknowledgments

I have many people to thank for the creation of this book. The bibliography suggests some of the authors and scholars who helped paved my way, kindred spirits and fellow admirers of L. M. Montgomery's work. Deep thanks to the estate of L. M. Montgomery for their gracious help and guidance. Thanks to the staff at the L. M. Montgomery Research Centre at the University of Guelph, who shared their time and resources, providing access to daybooks, journals, letters, and artifacts. Finally, I must thank the incomparable Mary Rubio, whose adult biography of L. M. Montgomery was an inspiration, and who was so giving of her time, energy, encouragement, and expertise.

I am forever grateful to my editor, Liz Bicknell, and the remarkable folks at Candlewick Press. To Paul Janeczko, for making the initial introductions. Thanks to the provost at Binghamton University and the dean of Harpur College for timely grants and support. And last but not least, I owe an eternal debt to my late husband, David Bosnick, who drove us all to Canada, and who, along with the rest of my family, lovingly tolerated the many hours I spent behind closed study doors.

None of this would have been possible without Maud herself. To quote the author, "Dead and in your grave, your charm is still potent enough to weave a tissue of sunshine over the darkness of the day. I thank you."